THE MAROONS IN NOVA SCOTIA

John N. Grant

Formac Publishing Company Limited
Halifax, 2002

Formac Publishing Company Limited acknowledges the support of the Cultural Affairs Section, Nova Scotia Department of Tourism and Culture. We acknowledge the financial support of the Government of Canada through the Book Publishing Industry Development Program (BPIDP) for our publishing activities.

We acknowledge the support of the Canada Council for the Arts for our publishing program.

National Library of Canada Cataloguing in Publication Data
    Grant, John N
        The Maroons in Nova Scotia / John N. Grant.
    Includes index.
    ISBN 0-88780-569-8
        1. Maroons—Nova Scotia. 2. Blacks—Nova Scotia—History.
    I. Title.
    FC2350.B6G73 2002   971.6'0049607292   C2002-903080-3
    F1040.N3G73 2002

Formac Publishing Company Limited
5502 Atlantic Street
Halifax, Nova Scotia
Canada B3H 1G4
www.formac.ca

Printed and bound in Canada

TABLE OF CONTENTS

DEDICATION

Because this topic has been part of my research interest for longer than the Maroons were in Nova Scotia, I am sure my family felt it might never be completed. I am, therefore, doubly pleased to dedicate this to my wife, Elizabeth, to my children, Julia, Heather, and Andrew, and to my mother, Jean Gardner Grant, (1911-2000).

August 2000 marked the 200th anniversary of the Maroon migration from Nova Scotia. This work is further dedicated to their indomitable spirit and pride of being.

ACKNOWLEDGEMENTS

Every work is the product of the contribution of many sources. Accordingly, I owe a debt of gratitude to a number of people and institutions and I hope I will be forgiven if I have not included all of them below. I first acknowledge the generous interest, or at least the grudging tolerance, of several years of students at the Nova Scotia Teachers College who were enrolled in my course on African-Canadian history. Likewise, I thank my former collegues and friends on the faculty and staff at the Nova Scotia Teachers College and my current co-workers in the School of Education at St. Francis Xavier University.

I also acknowledge the generous assistance afforded to me by the staff at the following archives, museums, and libraries: the Army Museum, Citadel Hill; the Art Gallery of Nova Scotia,; the Black Cultural Centre for Nova Scotia; the Colchester East Hants Regional Library (Elmsdale Branch), the Killam Library at Dalhousie University; the Dartmouth Heritage Museum; the Jamaica Archives; the Maritime Command Museum; the Maritime Museum of the Atlantic; the Nova Scotia Museum; the Nova Scotia Archives and Record Management; and the MacDonald Library at St. Francis Xavier University. Special thanks to David States, Garry Shutlak, Ron MacDonald, and Alan Marble for sharing information and resources with me, and to Bridglal Pachai, Ann Sherman, and Henry Bishop for their interest and support. A number of people have helped type and prepare the copy including Yvonne MacDougall, Connie Piers, Johanne Duggan, and Jennifer Callaghan and I appreciate their assistance. Special thanks to Debbie MacIsaac of the School of Education, St. Francis Xavier University, for her many, many hours of decoding, typing and correcting the manuscript and bringing it to a presentable state. Her skill and ability have made this task more possible. Barry Cahill, Senior Archivist of the Nova Scotia Archives and Record Management, read the entire manuscript for me and offered valuable advice and asked pertinent questions from which I have greatly benefited.

Thank you also to Mavis C. Campbell, whom I have never met, but who is frequently quoted herein and whose work is so appreciated. The support of the University Council for Research and that of the Centre for Regional Studies at St. Francis Xavier University were great spiritual as well as financial boosts. Thanks also to James Lorimer of Formac Publishing Company for undertaking the production and publication of this work and to Elizabeth Eve, Senior Editor, Formac Publishing; and to Sandra Barry, freelance copy editor, for their rigour and their guidance in bringing this work to its final form.

In 1803 R.C. Dallas, in the preface to his history of the Maroons, included a brief description of the tremulous times of the era in which he was working and concluded, "We have seen all the passions in a tempest, and nature herself struggling against the chaos which threatened her very existence." In the midst of such momentous events, then as now, why should a historian concentrate on the Maroons as an object of scholarship? Dallas responded to this question as follows: "The contemplation of stupendous objects, far from disqualifying the mind for the relish of less extensive views, heightens its satisfaction in them, as the eye, after pouring over the unbounded expanse of the ocean, is relieved and delighted by a streamlet and a dell." My justification is less poetic. I believe that the history of the Maroons is an important page in the history of Nova Scotia, one that has been greatly underestimated.

John N. Grant
Enfield, N.S.
2002

FOREWORD

When the exiled Trelawny Maroons of Jamaica arrived in Nova Scotia in 1796, Sir John Wentworth, the lieutenant-governor of the colony, provided them with uniforms, the buttons of which were etched with an alligator holding wheat ears and an olive branch, with the inscription "Jamaica to the Maroons 1796." Was Wentworth hoping that these strong-willed people would in time be tempered to a law-abiding, passive agricultural community? He certainly attempted to set up conditions to bring about this transformation of the Maroons, but their intensely independent spirit, which had rebelled in Jamaica, could not be subdued in Nova Scotia.

With this book Dr. John Grant offers the most comprehensive account to date of the Trelawny Maroons during their four years in Nova Scotia, 1796-1800. Since their sojourn was brief, historians have generally ignored the circumstances and experiences of the Maroons during this period, but it was a time and place significant in their ultimate destination and fate: their removal to and settlement in Sierra Leone. Moreover, their impact on the Nova Scotia Black community endured long after they departed.

By bringing together a wide range of primary and secondary sources, this book provides an in depth exploration of the context which brought the Maroons to Nova Scotia, of the conditions they experienced while there, and of the political, economic and psychological factors which caused their departure for Africa in 1800.

Nova Scotia was a bridge for the Maroons, from their Jamaican homeland, from which they were exiled, to the continent of their ancient ancestry, Africa. Though indeed brief, their time in Nova Scotia was more than simply a stop-over. By focusing on a remarkable group of people, whose presence in the province affected its politics at the highest level, and who had a lasting affect on the community in which they lived, John Grant's book fills a gap in Nova Scotia history.

Strong in mind and body, the Maroons, individually and collectively, were a formidable force. Descendants of the great Akan people of West Africa, possibly of the Ashanti nations, the Maroons were a warrior society. Free-willed and spiritually independent, with strong kinship ties, they struggled and rebelled against slavery, and Spanish and British persecution, for more than one hundred and forty years. Their tenacity, ingenious methods of combat, leadership skills and pragmatic acumen in negotiation were impressive. However, all these instincts and abilities, employed to refute and challenge colonial authorities, came with tremendous risks and costs, the ultimate being exile from their beloved, warm Jamaica, and arrival in an alien, cold Nova Scotia.

Even though the Maroons were for the most part actively disaffected for their entire stay in the colony, they nonetheless left their mark. The historical record is at best ambiguous about the precise numbers who arrived and departed. It would not have been in the interests of any of the parties — the Jamaican, Nova Scotian or British governments, or the Maroons themselves — to record officially that any of the Maroons remained in Nova Scotia after 1800. However, a strong oral tradition claims such was the case, and within the Black communities of the province today, echoes of the Maroons can still be detected.

Some of the family names in Black communities still connect to Maroon heritage: Smith, James, Colley, Williams, Brown, Downey, Gray, Johnson or Johnston, Thompson and Wright, to mention a few of the more common names current in the province. There are also the intriguing connections of African-Nova Scotian families, who are quite possibly descendants of the Maroons after their arrival in Africa (not all the Maroons ended up or stayed in Sierra Leone).

Fascinating as well are the trace memories of languages from the Caribbean region. The Maroons were multilingual, speaking a variety of dialects which are sometimes referred to as Creole, a language derived from a mixture of English and Spanish, with the Akan vernaculars. Within Black Nova Scotian communities today one can detect accents and word-phrasings which undoubtedly have origins in the

Maroon presence and influence.

Even after more than two hundred years there remain vestiges of family bonds among Maroon descendants. Customs and traditions have been retained despite racism and ridicule through the years. Even physical traits and trade skills continue to be passed on in the community. Most of all, the historical fact and mythology of a great people have endured in Nova Scotia; for example, in the practice of a close-knit community-based ideology, which was part of the survival technique developed by the spirited Maroon people living in the mountainous regions (the "cockpit country") of Jamaica, and carried with them to Nova Scotia. This belief in and commitment to a strong community is perhaps one of the most significant legacies of the Maroons.

The diaspora of African-descended peoples stretches around the world. It recrossed itself countless times during the past three centuries. The Maroons were a single river in these complex migrations (forced and free), but it contained many individual streams, some of which can be felt in Nova Scotia to this day.

Even though the majority of Maroon families opted to leave Nova Scotia and go to Sierra Leone, those few who stayed behind mingled and co-existed with other residents, spreading the bloodline across the region. The saga of the Maroons' arrival is compelling and remains of keen interest to all concerned with the early development of the province. Their story is filled with drama and mystery, unrest, political intrigue, hardship and severe weather. Dr. Grant's accurate and engaging retelling of this story is long overdue. This book is a valuable contribution to our better understanding of an important aspect of the African-Canadian experience. The stories of the past are necessary for the progress and future of any people.

Dr. Henry Bishop
Chief Curator
Black Cultural Centre for Nova Scotia
May 2002

CHRONOLOGY

March 1796: End of the last Maroon War (Trelawny Town).

June 1796: Maroons board transports in Jamaica bound to Halifax.

21-22 July 1796: Maroons arrive in Halifax.

August 1796: Maroon Town (Preston) settlement established.

Winter 1796-1797: Long hard winter spawns Maroon discontent.

23 April 1797: James Petition to Parliament seeking removal. Unknown to Wentworth but Ochterlony (and perhaps Quarrell) either aware or involved.

May 1797: Wentworth negotiated one more year with Maroons.

June 1797: Ochterlony fired. Alexander Howe in charge.

10 July 1797: Boydville settlement established.

22 July 1797: Quarrell resigns. Wentworth takes charge of Maroon settlement plan.

12 August 1797: 2nd James Petition to Parliament.

Winter 1797-1798: Second long hard winter faced by the Maroons.

March 1798: Wentworth received copies of Maroon petitions of 1797 from London.

9 July 1798: Howe replaced by Chamberlain. "Maroon Establishment" reduced.

22 July 1798: Jamaican government says no more support for Maroons.

July 1799: Wentworth receives orders from London that Maroons are to go to Sierra Leone.

October 1799: Ross, representative of the Sierra Leone government, arrives in Halifax.

31 May 1800: HMS *Asia* finally arrives in Halifax to transport the Maroons to Africa.

8 August 1800: Maroons set sail (about one year after government orders) to Africa.

30 September 1800: Maroons arrive in Sierra Leone.

Anyone who has worked with primary sources has likely wished that the records were more complete. Frustratingly, omissions are often in both the quantity and quality of the papers and in their author's comments. Furthermore, especially when dealing with the records of over two hundred years ago, files are often missing or incomplete, or the information needed today was of little consequence then, or so well known as to not warrant comment. In addition, while the writers were not necessarily withholding information from the researcher, there are times when one wishes that they were more forthcoming. Both the researcher and reader must realize that often the only, or least the majority, of available sources are official records — reports of government officials and other representatives of either the majority people or of those in power. While the "establishment" may not purposely misrepresent a situation or a minority group, they may nonetheless do so. Most of the reports on, or references to, the Maroons come from official reports. As most of the Maroons were unlettered (especially the elders), it is even difficult to take their petitions, letters, etc., at face value, or as being completely representative of their wishes and position, caught as the Maroons were in the political cauldron of the times.

The historian must also be careful not to read the attitudes of today into the meaning of the words of yesterday. Alternatively, one also has to be careful not to assume that these attitudes were not present. Wentworth, although a slave holder himself, was perhaps, according to Winks, remarkably free of racial bias, and Benjamin Gerrish Gray was, according to Campbell, remarkably understanding of the Maroons' desire to retain their cultural heritage. As both Wentworth and Gray lived in a time before the emergence of the scientific racism of the mid-years of the nineteenth century, their positions are perhaps not so remarkable. The social demarcation of their world was perhaps more one of class rather than of race, or some combination of class and race. This is not to suggest that most black people were considered to be other than lower class (as, indeed, were most white people), but because the military power of the British Empire was not absolute and native peoples were still necessary allies in many parts of the world, it was not yet accepted that they always had to be part of the lower class. The Maroons, some of whom had been slave holders in Jamaica, certainly would not have accepted the identification of race and class. However, the future would rate all Blacks as either being part of the lower class or at best an underclass which was outside of the class structure itself.

Secondary sources also reflect the prejudices of their authors. Many early sources deal with the Maroons and other black people with a bemused contempt, or at best detachment, or an amused affection, or exasperation. In their bemusement, authors exhibit both the accepted views of their times and likely their personal attitudes about race. While the historian cannot ignore these sources, they, like all the others, must be carefully sifted before they are used. Some of the sources carry other baggage. For example, Bryan Edwards is blatantly anti-Maroon, while Robert Charles Dallas is a strong advocate for his countryman W.D. Quarrell, to whom his two-volume work is dedicated. In both works objectivity was, no doubt, at times a victim to building a strong case. On the other hand Carey Robinson seems so enamoured of the Maroons' defiance that he may sacrifice objectivity as well.

Few of the over one hundred secondary sources listed in the Bibliography deal exclusively, or even primarily, with the Maroons. Being a peripheral rather than the central focus of these many historical accounts, little of the Maroon experience, especially in Nova Scotia, has been written within the "-ologies" or "-isms" of historical interpretation. One exception to this pattern is the work of Lennox O'Riley Picart. In his master's thesis and subsequent article, he interprets the Maroon experience within the conceptual framework of cultural survival and resistance to the forces that threatened it. While it does not sufficiently allow for the inconsistency of human nature, explain the division within the Maroon community, or acknowledge that the loudest voices do not necessarily represent the community the clearest, his is an interesting account and a worthy effort. The Maroon War of 1795-1796 has been examined within a Marxist theoretical framework. A.D. Dridzo, whose work I have read in translation, writing at the height of the Cold War, viewed the Maroon War as the consequence of a conspiracy of wealth designed to advance the interests of Jamaican landowners within the British Colonial power structure. While his work did not, to my knowledge, extend to the Nova Scotia experience, it would be an interesting extension of Marxist class warfare model. Robin Winks continues to provide the best short account of the Maroon experience in Nova Scotia, embedded within his synoptic work on the history of black Canadians. The many works of Mavis C. Campbell must be accorded a special place. Her history of the Maroon War of 1795-1796 provides more than simply a modern reworking of the sources, free of the political baggage of Edwards or Dallas. Her collation and careful analysis of the documentary sources is and will remain extremely valuable to researchers, and her articles reflect the extensive detective work required of modern historians of the eighteenth-century black experience. While not as admiring of her subject as Robinson, she obviously, with Robinson, influenced Picart's thesis. Campbell sees the Maroons as resisting colonialism and, undoubtedly, she has both a great sympathy with and admiration for the Maroons. However, her judgement has not been unduly clouded and her work is a faithful representation of their story.

For my part, I hope this work based on these sources will be useful to readers. Anything more must be left to the next generation of historians who re-examine the story of the Maroons.

J.N.G
Enfield, N.S.
May 2002

CHAPTER 1

Jamaica, Trelawny Town, War, and Exile

The Maroons were warriors. Described as "active, hardy and brave,"[1] as "masters of guerilla warfare"[2] and as "a troublesome, wild people,"[3] the Maroons were fiercely proud of their freedom and of their quasi-independent relationship with the government of British Jamaica. The origins of the Maroons are rooted deep in the history of that island. Lying green and white in the blue and gold of the Caribbean Sea, Jamaica was occupied by the Spanish by 1509 and was part of the first European colonial empire in the Americas. Only a small number of Spaniards settled in Jamaica, however, because "the riches of the American continent made [them] … neglect their West Indian Islands. Jamaica became the home of a few cattle ranchers whose production was infinitesimal compared with New Spain."[4]

Jamaica had no gold to satisfy the greed of its conquerors. Instead, Jamaica's ranches and farms became a source of supplies for the Spanish armies in the West Indies and in the Americas. The native Arawak Indians were enslaved by the Spaniards and African forced labour was introduced as early as 1517.[5] Because the Arawaks diminished in number very quickly,[6] the Spanish imported increasing numbers of enslaved Africans to take their place. They served as cowboys, herders and hunters, caring for the thousands of goats, pigs and cattle owned by the Spanish. These occupations allowed them a degree of freedom and an opportunity to become familiar with the forests and secret trails of Jamaica.

For over 140 years Jamaica remained part of the Spanish Empire. During many of these years, and especially toward the end, "the island was badly defended, poverty stricken, underdeveloped and underpopulated; the Government officials corrupt or weak and ineffective. The inhabitants were indolent and demoralized, money was scarce and trade was falling off."[7] In such a state the Spanish were not prepared to combat even the ill-disciplined English expedition sent by Oliver Cromwell in 1655 to capture nearby Hispaniola. While the fleet proved "inadequate for the task … they managed to take Jamaica" and the island became the first English colony to be gained by conquest.[8] When the 8,000 men from the 38 ships of the English fleet landed on 10 May 1655 the Spaniards abandoned their homes and defences "and fled to the mountains with their families" — a tactic which was "normal practice" whenever they were threatened by the raiders, buccaneers and pirates which were plentiful in the West Indies.[9] The Spanish took some of their slaves with them, while others seized the opportunity and fled to freedom in the wild hills of the limestone plateau in West Jamaica's Cockpit country where, "although the karst area does not encourage settlement, its inhospitabilness [sic] made it a good hiding place."[10] Unlike earlier raiders, the English had come to stay. They accepted the surrender of the Spanish governor and provided transports to carry the Spaniards from the island. Many left, but a hard core, led by Don Christoval Arnaldo de Ysassi, formed a resistance movement that fought the British conquerors until 1660.

The end of the Spanish resistance did not, however, bring peace to Jamaica. After 1655 the former slaves of the Spanish had enjoyed the freedom of the hills and while some had fought for Spain, others had fought only to be free. In 1663, when the British called upon them to come down from the hills, they refused to comply. Instead, they established their own settlements, learned the art of self-government and mastered the skills of guerrilla warfare. These were the original Maroons of Jamaica. Orlando Patterson points out,

> we do not … know where the original band of Spanish ex-slaves came from …. The great majority of the rebels during the British era were Coromantee or Akan-speaking slaves from the Gold Coast. Another important group were also the Papawas, or slaves from the Slave Coast (now

Dahomey). It is significant that the two major groups of rebels came from the areas of the Guinea Coast where the great West African empires of Ashanti and Dahomey were at that time [1730] at the height of their imperial expansion.[11]

The origin of the word "maroon" has been described variously, but the definition of a "fugitive slave who betakes himself to the woods"[12] is likely as useful as any. The term "maroon" was used generally and generically to describe a runaway, and "marronage" to describe the act and action of escaping slavery, whether temporarily or permanently.[13]

Under British rule and with the introduction of a superior quality of sugar cane, Jamaica prospered and became the wealthiest of the British West Indian Islands,[14] one of its most important colonies, and "His Majesty's prizest possession."[15] The economic importance of Jamaica to the Empire meant that it had to be protected from English buccaneers, from other Europeans, including Spain, Holland and France, and from raids by the Maroons. The sugar plantations that were the basis of this prosperity consumed large numbers of lives. On the plantations of Guiana, it was reported,

> In order to increase production, the slaves are driven to the breaking point. If they collapse under the burden, [the plantation owners] ... buy others .... In this manner, we have seen some plantations swallow as many as *four slave complements* in a period of twenty-five years.[16]

This almost insatiable appetite for labour continued to assure that most of Guiana's slaves were African born. Similarly, the mortality rate among slaves on Jamaican plantations was also very high. There were 40,000 slaves in 1690. Between 1690 and 1820, 800,000 were imported; but in 1820 there were only 340,000 slaves in Jamaica. Jamaica accordingly remained an important market for the West African slave trade. During the early years, the existence of the free and the enslaved in such close proximity meant that there were always slaves willing to risk their lives to swell the ranks of the Maroons:

> There were slave rebellions on the estates but they were punished by such cruel deaths, burning, hanging and breaking on the wheel, that it was some time before they spread. In Jamaica, however, there were at least twenty slave rebellions during the eighteenth century; one in 1760 spread to several estates, and sixty Europeans and four hundred negroes were killed before order was restored.[17]

Patterson argues, "Few slave societies present a more impressive record of slave revolts than Jamaica."[18]

Among those who escaped to the hills during a 1690 rebellion was a young Coromantee captive named Cudjoe, who led the Maroons in the ongoing raids against the British that were called the Maroon Wars. In 1738-39, however, the first series of Maroon Wars, which represented 84 years of almost continuous warfare, and had engaged three generations of Maroon warriors, came to an end. In March 1739, a peace treaty was agreed to by the government of Jamaica and by Cudjoe and his people. It acknowledged and guaranteed the full freedom of the Maroons and gave them control over specified sections of land. However, it also insisted that British superintendents would live in the Maroon communities and that the Maroons would both return runaway slaves and fight for the British King. These provisions, according to Jamaican historian Carey Robinson, were to change "the entire character of the Maroons and reverse their way of life." Robinson goes on to say:

> The Treaty was really a one-sided document. It gave the Maroons little that they did not already have, but it placed them under the jurisdiction of their late enemies who, while giving them the appearance of autonomy, really had final authority over their affairs. It also provided the colonists

with a ready-made and well-trained mercenary force to help them maintain the iron control necessary in a slave society. It was the triumph of a literate, sophisticated, cynical society motivated by expediency and gain, over an illiterate, vigorous, but simple community skilled only in warfare and physical survival.[19]

Thereafter, while occasionally the "Maroons disturbed the peace ... [they] did not directly effect [sic] estate discipline."[20] Nonetheless, theirs "was indeed a remarkable achievement of resistance. Here we have a group of free blacks during this early period of the colonial process who stoutly refused to have their lives fashioned by the dictates of their masters."[21] However, the Maroons soon proved to be useful to the English planters as slave catchers and as willing volunteers in the suppression of the occasional slave rebellion. As new colonial legislation continually restricted the freedom of the Maroons, slave catching was one of the few ways they could use their unparalleled ability as woodsmen and exercise their love of combat, and it offered both excitement and payment. In her comprehensive book, *The Maroons of Jamaica 1655-1796: A History of Resistance, Collaboration, and Betrayal,* Mavis C. Campbell points out, "Another service to the state for which the Maroons were paid was that of hunting down and returning runaways to their owners ... Ironically, this occupation soon became a most — perhaps the single most — important source of income to the Maroons." She adds that the runaways' "chances of being returned to an owner alive would be minimal — especially before mile money was paid for each returnee instead of his ears.... In addition to the prize money for each runaway returned, each Maroon party member was paid for the duration of the search in the woods."[22] Genovese notes:

The British authorities had no doubt that the military prowess of the Maroons was playing a major role in discouraging slave revolts. Moreover, although the treaty terms forbade the Maroons from owning slaves, they did buy some without provoking the intervention of the authorities. Maroons continued to marry slaves and to cultivate sympathetic relations with some, but increasingly the two groups diverged and passed over to animosity.[23]

Although the Maroons were sometimes suspected of hiding runaways and were known to find wives among the estate slaves, the respect and admiration that they had enjoyed from the slave population inevitably turned to hatred and fear.[24]

Trelawny Town, one of the five Maroon communities located in Jamaica, had been established by Cudjoe's original band. It was the Trelawny Maroons who eventually were settled in Nova Scotia. One of the leaders of Trelawny Town was Montague James, a true leader in war, resistance and peace in the tradition of better-known Maroon leaders like Cudjoe and Nanny. Likely of Ashanti or Akan descent, James emerged as a notable figure in the late 1770s or early 1780s. He was both captain and the assistant superintendent of Trelawny Town, the only Maroon to hold this commission. After years of loyal service to the colonial government that likely alienated him from his people from time to time, Montague James was removed from his position in the early 1790s in the movement that swept his superior and mentor, Superintendent Major James, out of office.

Fifty-seven years of peace between the Maroons and the Jamaican government came to an end in 1795 and it was the Trelawny Town Maroons who fought the last of the Maroon wars. The years of peace had limited the freedom of the Maroons, but had not affected either their pride or the way they felt about common slaves. Consequently, when two Maroons were convicted of stealing pigs and "whipped at the tail of a cart" in the presence of slaves and, even worse, at the hand of a runaway slave who had been recaptured by Maroons, the humiliation was complete. It was "a blow to Maroon pride and prestige and the whole Maroon community felt that they had been made the laughing stock of the slaves."[25] In consternation, the Maroons demanded of the authorities, "Do not subject us to insult and humiliation from the very

people to whom we are set in opposition."[26] This event, together with
an accumulation of ill-will, caused the Maroons of Trelawny Town to
drive the government superintendent from their community and leave
him with the impression that they were willing to fight.

Rumours and fears spread quickly among Jamaica's white minority.
The greatest fear of any slave-holding society was slave rebellion, and a
Maroon uprising was something to avoid if at all possible. Not only
would it mean that the Maroons' role as slave hunters and suppressors
of rebellion would be changed, but it could also provide a bad example
for the slave population. On Jamaica, where black slaves outnumbered
their white rulers by more than ten to one,[27] this imbalance was a real
danger. In addition, Britain and France were again at war. Jacobin
France had sent a fleet to the West Indies with a commander who used
slave rebellions as a means of recapturing lost territory. The fear arose
in Jamaica that French agents were exhorting the Maroons to attack the
British[28] as a first step in a general slave rebellion and an invasion by
the French forces.

Because of these fears, Alexander Lindsay, Earl of Balcarres, the
recently (April 1795) arrived governor ordered his last regiment of regular troops, which was enroute to Hispaniola, back to Jamaica and
declared martial law. Balcarres was an experienced and accomplished
military officer. Born in 1752, he succeeded to the peerage while in his
teens. His military career took him to various fields of combat. In 1775
he was a major of the 53rd Foot, then under orders to sail to Canada on
the outbreak of the American Revolution. In command of a battalion
of light infantry,[29] he demonstrated considerable ability as a military
leader.[30] In 1789 he was made colonel of the 63rd Foot and in 1793 was
gazetted major-general. He later commanded British forces in Jersey.
He was a Scots representative peer (1784-1825) and was Governor of
Jamaica from 1794 to 1801.

The over-reaction of the government to the Maroon dispute caused the
Maroons to believe the negotiations that had almost assured continued
peace had been undertaken in bad faith. As a result, on 12 August 1795,
the Trelawny Maroons burned their village and disappeared into the hills:

The Trelawny stood alone. They had received no help from the slave population, had been abandoned by their Accompong brethren and in addition were greatly outnumbered. They had a limited supply of food and gun powder and about two or three hundred fighting men. They were facing 1,500 regular troops supported by several thousand militia men who had access to unlimited supplies. In their favour the Trelawnys had a great tradition of courage and skill as guerilla fighters and an unsurpassed knowledge of the tremendously rugged countryside which their ancestors had used so well. They were also fortunate at this time of crisis in being able to produce first-class leaders. Having made up their minds to fight, they went into action immediately. [31]

And fight they did. Using the few advantages they had available to them, they staged ambushes, penetrated enemy lines, and emerged to fight again where they were often least expected. If faced by superior firepower, they simply withdrew and faded into the hills to await a better opportunity. Under the leadership of Montague James and Johnson, and captains John Jarrett, Smith, Dunbar, Leonard Parkinson, James Palmer, Charles Shaw and others, the Maroons moved in and out of the Cockpit County, which consisted of "500 square miles of land within the parishes of Trelawny, St. Elizabeth, and St. James,"[32] and inflicted serious losses on the local military. Campbell observes, "It appears that Montague [James] soon became the brains behind the revolt, leaving the more active combat to the younger men and women."[33] However, not even the leadership, skill, and bravery of the Maroons could prevent Lieutenant-Colonel George Walpole (promoted to major-general by Balcarres and in August 1795 put in charge of the campaign against the Maroons) from tightening the noose around their necks. Gradually, he "succeeded in limiting their food and water supply and appeared, if given time, to be on a victorious course."[34] Walpole, "by fighting the Maroons in their own way paved the way for their surrender."[35]

If overwhelming enemy forces, Walpole's howitzer, a lack of supplies, and an outbreak of measles were not formidable enough foes, the Maroons received word that they had to face an additional enemy. In the late fall of 1795 the Jamaican House of Assembly asked Lieutenant-Colonel William D. Quarrell to negotiate with the Spanish government of Cuba to procure dogs and their handlers used to hunt escaped slaves. On 17 December 1795, "forty Spanish chasseurs and 104 savage Cuban dogs landed at Montego Bay"[36] to be used to rout out the defiant Maroons. However, before the dogs and their handlers arrived on 21 December 1795 the Trelawnys had agreed to a truce:[37]

> The proposed peace terms were that the Maroons should beg His Majesty's pardon on their knees, that they should go to any place to which they were sent and settle on whatever lands the Government, Council and Assembly might think proper to allot them, and also that they should give up all run-aways. Walpole added a fourth, important term which was between the Maroons and himself and for which he took personal responsibility. He promised them that they would not be banished from Jamaica.[38]

Governor Balcarres ratified the Walpole-Montague James Treaty on 28 December 1795, and fixed 1 January 1796 as the date on which all the Trelawny Maroons should surrender.[39] Four days was, however, far too short a time to notify all the Maroon units scattered throughout the hills that they should come in. In addition, many of the Maroons found it difficult to overcome their distrust of Balcarres and his government. Consequently, the Maroons trickled, rather than rushed in to accept the conditions of their surrender. The various Trelawny units were eventually informed of the peace treaty and by March 1796 the last Maroon War was over.

Impatient with any delay, Balcarres ordered Walpole to again advance against the Maroons. Balcarres was determined to use every advantage to secure internal peace and restore civil order to Jamaica at a time when the entire British empire faced the threat of revolutionary France. Thus Balcarres "engineered for his own benefit the pretext of deporting them on the grounds of [their] having broken the treaty. To him, the final solution to the Trelawny Town Maroon was deportation."[40] Because the majority of the Trelawnys had not surrendered within the prescribed time and because very few runaway slaves had been recovered, the Governor declared that the terms of the treaty had been violated. Over the objections of General Walpole, who had given his personal and private word that the Maroons would not be deported, and those of his officers (who pointed out that Balcarres had privately agreed that surrenders could be accepted until 14 January),[41] but with the agreement of a special secret committee of members of the Council and Assembly of Jamaica, and with the approval of the Duke of Portland, the British secretary of state, Balcarres decided to get rid of the Trelawnys.

Balcarres' rank and lineage would suggest a person of a certain suavity and sophistication. However, Campbell contends:

> Balcarres kept one of the most dirty and depraved households in Jamaica. Lady Nugent, wife of Governor Nugent who succeeded Balcarres, was disgusted with his awful table manners, where with unwashed hands and dirty nails he would 'dip his fingers into every dish'; she was shocked by the dreadful 'scene of dirt and discomfort' at his residence. 'Never was there a more profligate and disgusting scene, and I really think he must have, been more than half mad.'. . . [His] favorite pet was a little black pig that had free run of the house.[42]

The Trelawny Town Maroons certainly never forgave Balcarres for their exile. Writing from Nova Scotia in 1797, Maroon Captain Andrew Smith asked his brother, Charles Samuels, who was then in England, to "Beg Massa King for no send any of dem Cotch Lord for Gubner again" (Ask the King not to send another Scotch lord to be Governor again).

The Jamaican Assembly, however, voted seven hundred guineas to present Balcarres with a sword to mark his contribution to the colony. Perhaps Alexander Lindsay, Earl of Balcarres, with the confidence of ancient rank and privilege, and sure of his duty, cared little for the opinions of Lady Nugent or the Maroons.[43]

The Maroons were moved from Montego Bay to Kingston to await their banishment, and they decided to face their future as they had shared their past. When some, who had surrendered prior to the treaty date, were told that they could stay, they asked to be allowed to share the fate of their brethren so as to remain together.[44] "A very telling example of Maroon attachment to family ties was demonstrated by those who were entitled to remain in the island — Smith, Dunbar, Williams, and the two boys who had surrendered before January 1." While the Assembly had also extended this allowance to some others, it would not offer it to their extended families and "both categories of Maroons petitioned finally to be allowed to accompany the others, and some fifty of them joined the fate of exile with their kinsmen." Because he could not keep his entire family in Jamaica, Smith accompanied them to Nova Scotia stating that "they must live and die together."[45]

The Maroons were not the only subject people of the empire to face deportation. Like the Acadians of Nova Scotia or the Caribs of St. Vincent, or indeed like many within the British Isles itself, the Maroons stood in the way of a peaceful and profitable imperial order. Like the earlier deportation of rebellious Highland Scots, and the later Highland Clearances, the "wave of deportations from the Caribbean in the latter part of the eighteenth century rested on two British preoccupations: heightened fears for security generated by the Napoleonic Wars in the region, and the colonial planters' perceptions of land scarcity."[46] In the face of these preoccupations, the Maroons, like the Highlanders, were expendable.

Balcarres was convinced that his decision to deport the Trelawnys had "saved the island," but Walpole was angry that his word had been broken. To express his anger and to demonstrate his contempt, he resigned his commission and refused to accept a gift of 500 guineas from the Jamaican Assembly, to purchase a sword of honour.[47] As early as July 1796 the *Halifax Journal* had informed its reading public of Walpole's refusal and noted, "[W]e understand a difference of opinion as to the observation of the Articles granted to the Maroons to be the cause."[48]

After this Walpole returned to England and was promoted to colonel. By this time he had been in the army 20 years having accepted his first commission in 1777 at 20 years of age. In 1795 he became lieu-tenant-colonel in the 13th Light Dragoons and went with the regiment to the West Indies. He entered politics in 1797 being elected to the House of Commons as MP for Derby (1797-1806), then represented Dungarvan (1807-1820). He became a vocal member of the radical Whig opposition led by Charles James Fox, serving as under-secretary at the foreign office (1806-1809) and then as comptroller of cash in the excise office for the rest of his life. Because he was chronically short of funds it "was supposed that Walpole needed parliamentary immunity from his creditors."[49]

After the decision to banish the Maroons was made,[50] the further decision of where to send them had to be addressed. Several destina-tions were considered, including Sierra Leone, the Bahamas, and Canada. Finally, Balcarres chose British North America and decided that Halifax, the forty-seven-year-old capital of Nova Scotia would be at least their temporary destination because British military transport ships that could take the Maroons there were leaving Jamaica:[51]

> On June 3 Balcarres wrote to the new Lieutenant-Governor of Nova Scotia, Sir John Wentworth, that he was sending the Maroons to Halifax in three transports, with provisions to follow. He asked neither Wentworth's permission nor his advice, and since he had decided six weeks earlier on this course of action, he clearly meant to present the Nova Scotian Governor with a *fait accompli*.[52]

Balcarres explained to Wentworth that "the very great scarcity of provisions, and the convenience of getting the Transports puts me under the necessity of sending them away to another port. I have therefore to request that they may be permitted to come to anchor at Halifax until his Majesty's pleasure is signified." He also informed Wentworth that the Jamaican Assembly had made it a felony for the Maroons to return to Jamaica. Moreover, apparently, slaves held by the Maroons were not to accompany them to Nova Scotia.[53]

In June 1796, 568 Maroons, "of whom 401 were old men, women, and children, 167 arms-bearing men,"[54] were marched aboard the transport ships, *Dover*, *Mary*, and *Ann*[55] and set sail for Halifax on 6 June 1796, in the company of a large fleet bound for Europe under convoy of HMS *Africa*, with *Reasonable*, *Iphigenia*, and *Scorpion*.

CHAPTER 2

Arrival in Nova Scotia

T he transports that brought the Maroons north carried more than the banished Trelawnys. The shipboard complement also included Commissary General William Dawes Quarrell and his deputy, Alexander Ochterlony (sometimes spelled Ochterloney), for whom streets in Dartmouth were later named.

William Quarrell was a wealthy planter and influential person. He was a member of the Legislative Assembly of Jamaica and served in the Maroon War. Though he was to suffer through illness and frustration in his commission with the exiled Maroons, he was rewarded by an appointment to His Majesty's Council of the Island of Jamaica. The Jamaican government later voted him £5,000 for his services in Nova Scotia and as compensation for his expenses and suffering.

Ochterlony was a Bostonian by birth but was always a British subject and may have been a loyalist emigré to Jamaica. There he apparently lived in Savanna LaMar and seems to have been a member of the Jamaican militia that saw action in the Maroon War. His appointment as Assistant Commissary-General to the Maroons in their exile to Nova Scotia suggests that he had either excellent qualifications or an influential patron, perhaps his friend Captain John Bailey, formerly of the 19th regiment of Light Dragoons and a merchant in Marthabrae. It was Bailey's ship that carried Ochterlony home to Jamaica after his removal from office in Halifax.

These two men were sent by the Government of Jamaica with a credit of £25,000 Jamaica currency to establish the exiles. Doctor John Oxley, who was appointed surgeon to the Maroons on 16 May 1796 by Balcarres, also accompanied the exiles.[56]

The voyage to Nova Scotia, as Robinson records,

took six weeks and the Trelawnys were quiet and well behaved. In spite of the surgeon, 17 of them died, which was small compared with the number of sailors and others who perished. During the voyage warm clothing was made for them out of linen, and this was cut in a uniform manner with a few distinctions to mark the officers.[57]

After parting with their escort along the American coast, the three transports, having been separated in the fog, arrived at Halifax on 21 and 22 July,[58] carrying approximately 550-560 Maroon men, women, and children.[59] Also on board was "the skeleton of the 96th or Queen's Royal Irish Regiment of Foot...as a guard" for the Maroons.[60] On their arrival "dozens of small craft converged on the lead ship, and from one emerged Prince Edward Augustus [later the Duke of Kent and Strathearn and Commander-in-Chief of His Majesty's forces in British North America] to provide a welcome to the city."[61] As Commander of the British forces in the region Edward inspected the Maroons clothed in their new linen uniforms while the band of the 96th Regiment played. He found that their "demeanour is lofty, their walk firm, and their persons erect"[62] and that they were "a smartly dressed body of men."[63] He was "impressed by the height, bearing and physique of the Trelawny warriors and thought that some use should immediately be made of their strength and vigour."[64]

The immediate fate of the Maroons was, however, in doubt as they were "only on sufferance until His Majesty's pleasure is known respecting their final destination."[65] In a dispatch dated 13 June 1796, the Duke of Portland asked Lieutenant-Governor Wentworth to "omit nothing in your power" to accommodate the Maroons "by supplying them with provisions and every other necessary that can alleviate the distress of their unhappy situation," but to do so only if it was "not inconsistent with the safety of the inhabitants of the Province." He further stated that he had hoped to prevent their transport to Halifax for "nothing could be further from the King's intentions to have them so disposed of."[66] On 15 July 1796 Portland informed Wentworth that, upon the "best consideration," for the present,

> the Maroons should be permitted to remain in Nova Scotia
> and until inquiry can be made, and information received, in
> regard to their being ultimately employed, if possible,
> under certain modifications and restrictions, either in the
> manner they themselves pray for, or in some other, where-
> by the public service may perhaps be benefited, or at least
> not endangered.[67]

On 23 July 1796 the *Weekly Chronicle*, which, like the other Halifax
newspapers, consisted chiefly of advertisements, news about the war,
official notices and declarations, North American and European copy,
and a minimum of local news, announced the arrival of the Maroons
"in six weeks from Jamaica" and of the "two Gentlemen, who are
appointed Commissioners to superintend the Settlement of the
maroons, on Lands in this Province."[68] The local concern that was
expressed about the Maroons, based on their reputation as a troublesome people, was abated by Commissioner Quarrell who apparently
was able to convince both the authorities and the "principal inhabitants" that there was nothing to fear from them.[69] Despite Quarrell's
assurances, Wentworth reported that "it is agreed that these people
remain on board the transports in the harbour, until His Majesty's
pleasure is communicated respecting them."[70] Circumstances soon dictated otherwise.

The war with France had continued unabated since 1793 and "the
French squadron under Admiral Richery was then off the coast, and it
was expected that he would visit Halifax. The fortifications at the
mouth of the harbour having fallen into decay were under repair, but
not sufficiently forward to afford protection in case of an attack."[71]
Consequently, Prince Edward, who had earlier warned the military
authorities that "the works upon the Citadel Hill will require very considerable repairs," became preoccupied with the refortification of
Halifax:[72]

Starting in 1795, spending on Halifax's defences soared; in that year alone, Prince Edward drew on the treasury for £100,000 and he continued to draw on the treasury for such amounts until Halifax's defences were transformed into an array of fortifications protecting the town and its seaward approaches. The collapsing fort on Citadel Hill was reconstructed, and Martello Towers ... were built at strategic locations. George's Island was fortified and new barracks built at the north and south sides of Citadel Hill. A severe labour shortage developed immediately, and Prince Edward turned to Wentworth to find the necessary workers, demanding the muster of six hundred militia.[73]

While the provincial militia had been used to repair Halifax's fortifications in 1793, 1794 and 1795,[74] Wentworth, pointing to the severe economic and agricultural ramifications of such a step, sought labourers elsewhere. Indeed, the availability of casual labour in Nova Scotia had been a concern since the 1792 migration of black loyalists to Sierra Leone.[75] The arrival of the Maroons provided at least a partial solution. Prince Edward reported:

> At the request of the two Commissioners, the Maroons were landed a few days after their arrival and disposed of in as comfortable a manner as could be done at the very short notice we had of their arrival, since which, at their own free will, and option, a part of them have been daily employed in the new works on the Citadel hill, at the same pay as His Majesty's troops.[76]

On 25 July 1796 Wentworth confirmed that "an arrangement has been concerted with His Royal Highness to relieve the Maroons from their confinement on board ship," a move, which he later stated, "preserved them from an infection that has since appeared ... on board the *Dover*."[77] Wentworth further reported:

Probably about one hundred and fifty men will engage, and thereby release some of the inhabitants to assist in the harvests, and other civil occupations, which are now distressed for want of hands. The greatest care will be taken to preserve peace and good order among these people who seem perfectly well disposed, insomuch that there is not any cause to apprehend the least inconvenience, but, on the contrary, that very salutary effects will be derived from this measure.[78]

The arrangement concerted with Prince Edward, which employed them "voluntarily, as Labourers on the Fortifications erecting here at 9d per diem — provisions, lodging and clothing found for them," demonstrated the immediate usefulness of the Maroons to the province. It was also likely equally useful to the Maroons as it supplied them with jobs and income. In addition, their employment as labourers on Fort George, Prince Edward's modification of the earthworks of Citadel Hill, meant that their memory was perpetuated by reference to the Maroon Bastion.[79]

CHAPTER 3

The Creation of Maroon Town

L ocal concerns about the "dreadful banditti"[80] altered, or at least abated. While it is likely that some of the Maroons employed by government lived in "wooden barracks and tents that were set up for them near the citadel,"[81] most were "lodged about two miles from the town, with tolerable convenience to themselves, separate from the inhabitants."[82] Perhaps this separation, "by my Advice, and under my daily Inspection," the assurances of Quarrell, the "quiet and orderly"[83] behaviour of the Trelawnys, their employment and the subsequent salary they had to spend locally, and "the respect that a frontier and sea-going community naturally gives to brave men,"[84] helped to win their, likely conditional, acceptance by the community. Prince Edward, who seems to have approved of the Maroons, stated:

> It is but justice to them to say that they conduct themselves in the most orderly and obedient manner and that whatever may have been their former errors, they now seem fully determined to do their utmost to merit His Majesty's favour and forgiveness.[85]

Sir John Wentworth's efforts on behalf of the Maroons was one of many of his many memorable and significant achievements as lieutenant-governor. Born in Portsmouth, New Hampshire, he graduated from Harvard College and was subsequently employed in his father's merchant firm. He was in London when his uncle, Benning Wentworth, was removed from office and John Wentworth succeeded to the positions of Governor of New Hampshire and Surveyor-General of the King's Woods in North America. He remained loyal to Britain

41

during the Revolution and, as a consequence, was forced to leave his birthplace and family home. He continued as surveyor-general responsibilities from Halifax while his English cousins and personal connections, especially Charles Watson-Wentworth, the Marquess of Rockingham, lobbied the government in London for his advancement. He became lieutenant-governor of Nova Scotia in 1792 and was made baronet in 1795. He enjoyed a personal friendship with Prince Edward Augustus and made extensive use of his own patronage to create an extensive sphere of influence in Nova Scotia. He saw little difference between dissent and disloyalty and had little sympathy for those who disagreed with him. This intransigence was partly responsible for the opposition expressed by the Nova Scotia Assembly to his plans to settle the Maroons in the province.[86]

Certainly Wentworth very quickly became convinced that the Maroons should stay in Nova Scotia and employed. Some went to work at Government House where they "were paid at the rate and clothed in the manner of English Servants of their class … to remove all kinds of prepossessions against them from the minds of the inhabitants; and at the same time give encouragement and comfort to the Maroons."[87]

Brian Cuthbertson notes that in 1796 "Wentworth was at his zenith as Governor of Nova Scotia. He felt supremely equal to the challenge of turning the warlike Maroons … into peaceful farmers in the healthier, cooler climate of Nova Scotia."[88] Wentworth, who "seems to have been genuinely free of racial bias,"[89] was able to convince William Quarrell and Alexander Ochterlony of the wisdom of his plan to settle the Maroons in Nova Scotia.[90] Wentworth moved quickly to carry it out. As early as 15 July 1796 the Duke of Portland had instructed Wentworth,

> Adopt your own means as local circumstances, and your own wisdom shall point out to you, as most expedient for carrying it into effect, and for disposing of these people within the Province, in such manner as may most effectively enforce their quiet and peaceful behaviour, secure his Majesty's Subjects from any just cause of alarm, and may, at

the same time, best enable the Maroons to support themselves by their own labour and industry.[91]

Within a month Wentworth reported the action taken by the
Jamaican agents. "By my advice and information," he wrote, "they purchased several estates within five miles of this town" in an area
Wentworth knew well. When Sir John and Lady Wentworth surrendered

> their Bedford Basin retreat to Prince Edward, the
> Wentworths had bought an estate and built a summer resi-
> dence on a Preston hilltop, commanding a magnificent
> view of lakes and streams and rolling wooded hills. Here
> they entertained royalty, saluting the approach of distin-
> guished guests such as the prince and Madame with the
> boom of a cannon on the terrace and maintaining a staff of
> well-trained servants, white and black.[92]

To underscore both the good intentions of the Maroons and their
attachment to him, Wentworth reported that "50, or more of them at a
time ... have ... without any cost to the concern, been accommodated
in the offices at Sir John Wentworth's farm, where he occasionally
resided."[93]

The deserted farms at Preston had been vacated by black loyalists
who had fled "Nova Scarcity" for Sierra Leone in 1792 and by white loyalists who had similarly decided to test their fate elsewhere. The nearly
3000 acres with their buildings and necessary repairs, were expected to
cost approximately £3000 sterling. Wentworth explained that part of
the land was already cleared for cultivation, and that the uncleared por-
tions would provide the Maroons with all the necessary firewood.
Furthermore, the houses already standing, "with eight or ten more,
which we can erect immediately and commodiously, can warmly lodge
them for the ensuing winter, and before any cold weather can bother
them."[94] This was, no doubt, a fortuitous sale for the owners, who

would not likely have done so well on the difficult Nova Scotian real estate market. Undoubtedly, "pecuniary motives of Halifax merchants were also behind the desire to have the Maroons settle in Nova Scotia,"[95] as the £25,000 of credit on the government of Jamaica that Quarrell commanded was a powerful attraction.

Despite Wentworth's assurances that he intended "to have the whole of them settled by Michaelmas [29 September]," and that "these people express great delight in the country, and the prospect of being settled in it," and that "they are perfectly quiet orderly and peaceable, and I have not a doubt but that they will be more happy than ever they were in Jamaica,"[96] there were those who worried about how the climate would affect the Maroons. In September 1796 the Duke of Portland had received a warning "that the removal of the Maroons to Halifax is little short of national murder, and that it would have been more humane to have put these people ... to death in Jamaica ... than to keep them in the rigorous climate of Nova Scotia during the ... winter."[97] Portland apparently shared this concern and warned Wentworth,

> that in regard to the measures which may be adopted for their permanent establishment much will depend on your report to me how far the climate of Nova Scotia is, or can, by the help of such means as your attention and humanity will lead you to adopt, be rendered unhurtful to the temperament and constitutions of the Maroons.[98]

Wentworth, based on his experience in both New Hampshire and Nova Scotia, hastened to assure Portland that, with the proper food, shelter and clothing, even "Negroes directly from the hottest coasts of Africa have grown strong and lusty and in the winter, that they did not suffer by it."[99] Wentworth insisted that any apprehension about climate was specious and under carefully managed conditions the Maroons would be healthy and prosperous.[100] Dr. John Oxley concurred, reporting, "On their first landing in July last year, we met with many losses, principally, owing to their long Confinement on Board of the Ships, and the Badness of the water about the Blue Bell occasioned by the great Drought at that Time." Thereafter, they were "very well until February and March, when we had much sickness, chiefly Pleurisies and Sore Throats, but from which most of them recovered."[101]

Meanwhile, the settlement of the Maroons proceeded apace. In mid-August some of the families were moved "to their respective habitations,"[102] but it proved to be impossible to house them individually before the onset of winter. During the late summer, Wentworth reported that "about 50 of them sleep in my Outhouse at the Farm where I am often without a sentry or even locking a door or window."[103] By mid-September, in preparation for a winter that was expected to be "cold with more snow than usual," the Maroons were "all settled in comfortable good Houses,"[104] although "there are more in each house than would be expedient — owing to the want of materials and artifices to build more before the winter commenced." This was a condition Wentworth hoped to correct "by removing them in families into separate houses and farms annexed as soon as the ensuing season admits."[105] Nonetheless, Wentworth "was persuaded they will honestly perform, with quite as few Deviations as we should find in an equal number of more enlightened White People, from any Part of Europe or America, and far more easily reformed."[106]

The settlement was not made without some difficulty. The lengthy list of supplies that Wentworth had ordered from English merchants did not arrive until long after they were needed[107] and goods had to be purchased in the more expensive Halifax market, which cut deeply into the £25,000 of Jamaican credit. There was also some dissatisfaction expressed by the Trelawnys themselves. Despite Wentworth's assurances that they were "very peaceful, orderly and entirely inoffensive,"[108] and that they all "have full confidence in me," he admitted on 10 October that "a few men among them only appear to be ill tempered and dissatisfied."[109] These few, who apparently were displeased with the "priority of removal and choice of habitation,"[110] were, however, "all fully sensible of their utter inability to any Military opposition, and by far the greatest part of them being sensibly inclined to make the best of their situation, that the rest must submit — and in a very little time be as well pleased."[111] While it was not possible to identify it as such at the time, the future would show that this initial dissatisfaction by a few was an omen of things to come. Another difficulty, which was to develop in the future, was a disagreement about how the Maroons should be settled in Nova Scotia. Quarrell, who had been "attacked by a fever, for the third time since he left Jamaica, and ... confined to his bed,"[112] was ill during much of his early term in Nova Scotia, and remained "much indisposed with a gouty bilious complaint."[113] Quarrell's illness had allowed Wentworth to seize the initiative and to put his own settlement plans into effect. While Quarrell had consented to the Preston purchases, and was "ever delicate on giving my advice against any measures Sir John Wentworth determined on,"[114] he was apparently not convinced that keeping the Maroons together was the best way to integrate them into the community. He "came to the conclusion that the only way to get the Maroons to adopt a European way of life was to break up their community and scatter them among the white inhabitants."[115] Quarrell, according to his confidant Dallas, "freely communicated to the Assembly of Jamaica his sentiments respecting the proceedings with the Maroons, stating the impolicy of keeping them in a body, and predicting that the island would not be soon released from the burden of supporting them."[116] Here he ran directly contrary to the wishes of Sir John, who saw no reason why his plans to turn the Maroons into peaceful farmers would not succeed. It is unclear just when Deputy Commissioner Alexander Ochterlony's own plans for the Maroons developed, but he, too, would come to disagree with Wentworth about their fate.

CHAPTER 4

Halifax at War

In the 1790s Halifax was not yet fifty years old — still a city in the making. The streets were thronged with soldiers, sailors, French prisoners-of-war, Mi'kmaq, German market gardeners, American traders, and African-Nova Scotians, both slave and free. Halifax owed its creation and existence to its strategic military position and its prosperity ebbed and flowed on the tides of the military presence. Parts of the community were rough and unfettered and there were those who claimed that "Halifax was garrisoned by 'one regiment of artillery, two of infantry and three of whores'."[117]

The entire account of the Maroons in Nova Scotia lies within the context of the war that put Britain and her allies in conflict with revolutionary France. From 1793 to 1815, with two intermissions, Britain and France faced off in a world-wide struggle for political, economic, and military dominance. The war was felt in every outpost of the empire and Halifax took on the character that would earn it the Kiplingesque designation, "Warden of the North." "Wartime trade and privateering occasioned a general return to prosperity. The capital, and especially the Wentworth household, glittered with the social events attending the frequent visits of Edward Augustus, commander-in-chief in Nova Scotia."[118] For those who were in a position to take advantage of the ongoing war with France, it was a time of prosperity — a prosperity demonstrated by the splendid residences, country estates, and flourishing business houses of the gentry. Inns and coffee houses like the Golden Ball, Great Pontac and Spread Eagle (known locally as the Split Crow) were filled with customers. There was, however, a darker side to the gay life of Halifax society. All classes lived in fear of disease and the old town was filthy, riddled with pestilence, and offering every known vice to those who could afford it.

Henry Alline, the Nova Scotia evangelist of the New Light Movement, writing of his visit to Halifax in 1783, stated: "I preached in different parts of the town and have reason to believe that there were two or three souls that received the Lord Jesus Christ. But the people in general are almost as dark and vile as Sodom."[119]

Even though Prince Edward "took a stern view of drunkenness and even, according to contemporaries, made an inexorable stand against the loose morals of society at large,"[120] there is no reason to believe that the 1790s had significantly changed the character of Halifax, which was considered by some as the "top contender for the title Sink of Iniquity."[121] Because of the war with France, "press gangs harried the town, searching taverns, brothels, and frequently the homes of townsmen"[122] in search of fresh recruits — cannon fodder for the Royal Navy.

While there is no evidence that any of the Maroons were pressed into the Navy, among Wentworth's plans for the Maroons, whom he felt would be "decidedly good Men against any Enemy,"[123] was their potential military use if the province was attacked by France. Wentworth had established the Royal Nova Scotia Regiment, which had blacks recruited as pioneers (and a black company formed part of the 1st Battalion of the Halifax militia), and he felt that the Maroon warrior tradition would make them a useful addition to the defence of the colony.[124] Wentworth was insistent that everyone would participate in the defence of the province, and wrote that "if any man refused this just testimony of loyalty and love of his country — whether Indian, Acadian, British or Blackman, let him depart to Old France, whither I will certainly send him."[125]

In late September, when renewed fears of invasion were aroused by a French squadron's attack on the harbour of Bay of Bulls in Newfoundland, Wentworth assured Portland that the defence was ready.[126] In Halifax he had "seven hundred good Militia who may be depended upon." In addition, there was "another select regiment [the Royal Nova Scotia Regiment] of one thousand men, commanded by half-pay officers, and composed of privates, most of whom served under these officers during the late war. They have two companies of Artillery and one of Horse, and can be assembled in Halifax in six days' notice, part of them sooner." There were also three regiments in the western part of the province, one of which included the once expelled, now returned and welcomed Acadians.[127] In addition to the regular troops and the militia, Wentworth explained that "the Maroons are much attached to [and] impressed with hatred to the French" and could be counted on. However, in the case of both the Maroons and the Indians, "altho' they may be hence safely trusted, yet their wives and children to whom they are extremely attached being pledges for their fidelity, they will be advantageously employed more immediately under my own inspection, and with a Company of Riflemen, who are equal to either Maroons or Indians in the woods, and difficult rocky country."

The Maroons, however, needed no threats or "pledges for their fidelity" to encourage them to fight. Indeed, they looked forward to action. Maroon Captain Andrew Smith may have expressed the views of many of his fellows when he stated:

> [T]hey talk of the French coming here, if they do we are to be employed against them and by Heaven cold as the weather may be we will warm them every step of the road they take towards Halifax[,] we shall offer our service in a Body to the Prince who treats us as if he had confidence in us, we are all anxious for an opportunity of shewing him that we are and ever will be a brave and loyal people and will die in defence of him, our King or his good family.[128]

The Maroon tradition of a semi-military form of government in a quasi-independent relationship with the central authority was, at least in form, maintained in Nova Scotia. First, the Trelawnys were settled together in a community, with resident superintendents, a political organization which was reminiscent of the system in the Maroon towns in their far away Jamaican homeland. Second, during a meeting of the Maroons on 18 September 1796, "some arrangements were directed for

their internal good order and peaceable demeanor." These "arrangements" were designed "so as to lead them gradually into the general
operation of the Laws of the Province." Wentworth explained:

> The principles of these rules are — that all small offenses
> are to be openly tried before Mr. Quarrell, or Mr.
> Ochterlony — in presence of at least three Maroon
> Captains, and if fully proven, the offender to be delivered
> over to them, informing them what would be the sentence
> of the law, if the case arose between white men, explaining
> the good that might be expected from adopting the same.
> As their former habits led to severe punishments I have
> decided that those of any cruel proportion should be sus-
> pended until the case was reported to me by the commis-
> sioners and the Captains who were at the trial.[129]

This, too, was somewhat reminiscent of their Jamaican tradition in
that it allowed the Maroons at least the semblance, if not the reality, of
power. Third, and again in the Maroon tradition, the Lieutenant-
Governor appointed captains and majors among them; "the higher
rank of Colonel was bestowed on Montague James" who was the last
chief of the Trelawny Town Maroons, the assistant-superintendent of
Trelawny Town, and a principal actor in the events that led his people
first to Nova Scotia and then to Sierra Leone.[130]

In the tradition of the uniforms that had been made aboard ship
prior to the Maroons' arrival in Halifax, Wentworth ordered officers'
uniforms for them, including "handsome coats and vests, cocked hats,
scarlet clothing, and gold lace."[131] Among the myriad supplies
Wentworth ordered, such as seeds for seventy gardens, grid irons, cloth,
pipes, thimbles, handkerchiefs, spoons, pothooks and chopping hatch-
ets, there was also "40 gross coat and 60 gross vest," strong white metal
buttons emblazoned with "an alligator holding wheat ears and an olive
branch ... [and the] inscription Jamaica to the Maroons 1796." While
no doubt utilitarian, as they were to "be larger and of a quality fit for

labourers," [132] these clothes and uniforms were intended to remind the Trelawnys of the largesse of the Jamaican authorities, and help them maintain the traditional structures of command, which led of course, to Wentworth himself. [133]

CHAPTER 5

Education and Religion

While seeing to the settlement and governance of the Maroons, Wentworth was also concerned about their spiritual and educational needs. This concern was to be a challenge — a challenge he was prepared to accept. Bryan Edwards commented in 1796 that the Maroons

> are in general ignorant of our language, and all of them are attached to the gloomy superstitions of Africa (derived from their ancestors) with such enthusiastick [*sic*] zeal and reverential ardour, as I think can only be eradicated with their lives ... believing the prevalence of *Obi* ... and the supernatural power of their *Obeah* men. Obstacles like these ... few clergymen would, I think, be pleased to encounter lest they might experience all the sufferings, without acquiring the glory of martyrdom.[134]

Because the Maroons "worshipped false gods, and knew nothing whatever of Christianity, on their arrival in Nova Scotia,"[135] Wentworth felt it necessary to encourage their conversion, and as they were generally illiterate, he determined they should have the opportunity to learn to read and write. He argued that "among the best means to advance their civilization is immediate instruction in the Christian religion, reading, writing and arithmetic."[136]

He requested the sum of £240 sterling per annum, which he felt would "reclaim them to the Church of England, and disseminate Christian piety, morality, and loyalty among them and prove the most beneficial charity ... and ... blessing unto them."[137] In mid-October 1796 the Duke of Portland assured the Lieutenant-Governor that he would quickly determine if clergy could be made available to the Maroons,[138] but by then Wentworth had already acted with his usual precipitous enthusiasm. On 20 September 1796, he explained that because the Maroons "earnestly expressed their wishes to be instructed in our religion and to have their children taught to read and write," and with the agreement of Quarrell and Ochterlony, he had appointed Benjamin Gerrish Gray to be chaplain and teacher to the Maroons, with the help of an assistant. Wentworth had also arranged for the "shell of a large house nearly central in the settlement ... to be made convenient for a chapel,"[139] which he opened on 23 October by attending worship there. This building also housed the school, which commenced the following day.[140] While his duties within the Maroon establishment occupied most of Gray's time,

> [he still] had to minister to the other three quarters of the parishioners, most of them being outside the Preston area. In his 1796-1797 report to the S.P.G. Gray wrote that he had ninety-five families in the parish: forty-eight Church of England, twenty-five Roman Catholic, twelve Presbyterian, five Quaker and four Sandemanian.[141]

Wentworth had persuaded both preacher and teacher to move, with their families, into the settlement so that they could, by both precept and example, guide the Maroons.[142] In December 1796, Wentworth reported his success:

> Every Sunday public worship is performed in the church by the Rev. Mr. Gray, which is attended with great decency and desire of instruction — several are baptized, and some married, under engagements to avoid polygamy. The school is also daily attended by the children, under the instruction of Mr. Chamberlain, a man of education and excellent principles, peculiarly qualified having formerly been a teacher to the Indians in the wilderness of America.[143]

Theophilus Chamberlain, born in Northfield, Massachusetts, was at various times during his long life a soldier, justice of the peace, surveyor, teacher, Congregational Minister, Sandemanian Bishop, administrator and farmer. An avowed loyalist, he came to Nova Scotia in 1783 and was among those, both white and black, who received a land grant in Preston, where he lived until his death. A friend of Wentworth and other government officials, Chamberlain was entrusted with responsibilities in each of the three major migrations of black people to Nova Scotia: the loyalists, the Maroons, and the refugees of the War of 1812. In addition to his duties as school teacher, he was also overseer of the surveying and allotment of land and, later, superintendent. His great concern was for the advancement of the interests of his beloved Preston, which he had named, and for his family and fellow Sandemanians of whom he was the acknowledged leader.[144]

In May 1797, after a difficult winter, Wentworth again approached Portland for "support of the Missionary, or Chaplain, and Schoolmaster." The Maroons, he declared, "still attend public worship on Sundays; and twice a week, they go to the clergyman for explanations and instruction on the service of the preceeding Sunday, and the children constantly at School learning to read and write, with decency and diligence."[145]

Several examples of the work of the scholars at the Maroon school, which Wentworth had proudly commended to London, have survived. John Thorpe, when a Maroon Town school boy, "transcribing in his best script," wrote:

> God gives us the greatest Encouragement to be good, by promising us more Happiness than we can express, or all the World can afford, and he also declares, that if we continue in Sin, and disobey him, he will punish us forever, and ever. If then, neither these Promises nor Threatenings will do, we are unavoidably lost. — Pitch upon such a Course of Life as is excellent and praise worthy. - *John Thorpe, Maroon School Preston, August 15, 1799.*[146]

In *Back to Africa, George Ross & the Maroons: From Nova Scotia to Sierra Leone*, Mavis Campbell contends "The precepts involved, were meant, no doubt, to equip the young man with a new point of view since the *old* Maroons had stoutly refused to be handicapped by Christianity or by British education while in Nova Scotia, but they did not object to the *young* being so socialized."[147]

At least, during good times, they did not object. Wentworth noted that when they had grievances or resentments "they desist from Church, and take the children from school. The sign of their yielding, is returning the boys to school, and going to Church on Sunday."

Reverend Gray had a clear view of the place of education in the community. He hoped it would be used to stop

> the progress of their degeneracy and for impressing purer habits upon the rising generation — and this was particularly the object of instituting a public school in which, with the Element of Letters, the children would insensibly imbibe true ideas of Loyalty and Piety, and be confirmed in the love of those useful impulses, Filial Duty, Brotherly Affection, and universal Charity — I have found ... their desire of Education strong and they could ... make rapid advances ... if the unfortunate Engagements of their Fathers, did not lead them rather to check than encourage there [*sic*] attachment to it.[148]

Gray had asked the Society for the Propagation of the Gospel (SPG) for books for his poor parish and they responded by sending him "three dozen copies of Dixon's Spelling Book, two dozen copies of Crossman's Introduction, two dozen Psalters, twenty-five Prayer Books and twelve Bibles." When he finally received the materials in the spring of 1799, "he decided to loan the Bibles to the Christian Maroon youth, whom he reported to be making great progress both in education and in Christian faith."[149] Wentworth praised the success of the school, which, like the Church, was supported by the SPG, and the "fidelity and other merits of Mr. Hutchins, the School Master [in 1799], whose virtuous example is not less useful to them." He explained that the class had been maintained at nineteen because "we do not think it advisable to admit too many into School, until this class are so well forwarded, as to aid, rather than impede instruction," then the number would immediately be increased to twenty six, "and afterwards increased gradually, so as to have all instructed in time." Wentworth's pleasure with "the enclosed specimens of writing [which] will afford some estimate of the success of the school," also extended to the "Scholars, who were examined in the public Church on Easter Sunday, they repeated the Catechism, Creed, Lords Prayer and Commandments with admirable precision, and read all the lessons and responses during the Service, correctly."[150]

The Maroon school attracted visitors, among them Prince Louis Philippe, Duc d'Orleans, who was exiled from France during many of the years of the Republic and the Emperor Napoleon's rule. While visiting Halifax in 1797, he taught a lesson in Chamberlain's school.[151] Schooling, as a means "of reclaiming these people," or at least the boys, was continued on board the *Asia* en route to Africa and later in Sierra Leone.[152]

Wentworth argued, "I anticipate the greatest benefits to these people, and am fully justified in such expectations from the progress already made."[153] Sir John's expectations of conversion to Christianity, however, were largely frustrated. While education might eventually make an impression on the young, the adult generation, as Dr. Oxley warned Wentworth, "will ever be Maroons,"[154] and they were ever strong in their traditions and their religious beliefs. To Christian colonials and colonial officials the most glaring and grating manifestations of these were the Maroons' practice of polygamy and their burial customs.

The practice of permitting a man to have more than one wife was tied to his ability to provide for their well-being.[155] It was a practice "they always refused to abandon, nor did they approve of the performance of any marriage ceremony, and when pressed to forego the former they generally retorted, by making insolent observations, on the latitude in which some of the greatest known to them had indulged."[156]

The latitude, specifically Sir John Wentworth's (as well as that of Ochterlony and his friends), left little room for moralizing. Moreover, while the Maroons might have had problems understanding the language of the sermon,[157] they obviously grasped enough of the theology to pose awkward questions to the clergy, such as, "if, we must abandon one or another of our wives, and children, which should it be? Would it not be sinful to cast off these beloved responsibilities?" Answers, of course, other than resorting to the admonition "to forsake all others but her,"[158] were in short supply. Perhaps partly in jest, "at one point the Maroon men agreed to be faithful to one woman, if the other women would agree to it." There was little risk in this proposition because the men were sure that "none of the women would concede to any agreement that would jeopardize the men's responsibility to provide for their children."[159] Later, following their migration to Africa, the government of Sierra Leone also tried, with about the same degree of success, to stifle polygamy. The practice continued into another generation of Maroons and did not end until the 1830s.[160]

The funeral practices of the Maroons were also contrary to the habits and customs of Nova Scotia. In 1829 Thomas C. Haliburton noted "[W]hen a Maroon died, he was buried with the Coromantie ceremonies."[161] Lennox Picart, generally employing the 1803 work of R.C. Dallas, also made note of their burial practices:

> While they lived on the Preston estate, they continued to conduct their burials in the Coromantie rituals. The deceased was simply taken to a place of rest where he/she would then be buried under a heap of stones. Various articles that were deemed necessary to help the individual on the voyage to the other world were buried as well. The usual articles included such things as a bottle of rum, a pipe and tobacco, and two days' food rations. Singing … was part of the service [and] … it might have been ancient African burial songs the Maroons were chanting during their funerals, which would explain why Nova Scotians found them perplexing.[162]

This description echoes many of the rites that were also part of slave funerals in Jamaica in these same years and "show close affinities with funeral rites described in West Africa," which included references to "sing and Howie [sic] in a sorrowful manner in their own language" and the placing of "Casavar bread, Roasted Fowles, Sugar, Rum, Tobacco and Pipes with fier [sic]... to sustain him in his Journey beyond." Drumming was part of the ceremony because of its importance "as a means of summoning other ancestral spirits to participate in the funeral rites," while songs "addressed to the spirit persuaded it to act favourably towards the living." In slave funerals, and perhaps for the Maroons, the belief developed that "the journey" was the return of the spirit "to Africa and the new custom of sending greetings, via the spirit, to relatives in Africa." For the exiled Maroons, however, probably the journey was a return to their lost Jamaica.[163]

Mavis Campbell also commented on the funeral practices of the Maroons, who were, for the most part, originally of the Akan speaking group of Ghana.[164] She notes in her work on the Ross diary:

> R.S. Rattery, in his careful works on the Ashanti people, established that rum was indeed served on funeral occasions, but this was followed only after all concerned had fasted throughout the day and as a considerable quantity of liquor was consumed the effect of this showed on a number of people. Much of the intoxication noticed by Europeans on such occasions ... is due to the fact that those participating have been fasting for long periods, so that even a little liquor soon goes to the head. Moreover, indulgence on such occasions only takes place after the solemn rites have been performed and after all the serious business of the day is over.[165]

Superintendent George Ross noted the funeral ceremonies of the Maroons. While pondering on the drunkenness at a funeral, he wrote in his diary, "You will have drumming over your daughter, tho' I don't consent to it!" and "Drunken Bailey — to my no small annoyance got sluttering Elliott to chant over the corpse before burial." However, he also noted, "Tis true that at the desire of the Maroons I read prayers over the grave — much the better for that no doubt!"[166] Whether this admission of Christian prayers was a diplomatic gesture to Ross and the government of Sierra Leone or an early indication of religious change is difficult to measure. They had certainly not been permitted in Nova Scotia where, according to Robin Winks:

> They listened to the various ministers of religion who moved among them 'with contumely'. They persisted in holding to plural wives, and to their burial customs, which seemed bizarre and unhealthy. They were given to swaggering about in their military garb, arrogant, rude, heathenish, and superstitious.[167]

Kenneth M. Bilby points out that there is "little in the historical literature from which we can draw a picture of the traditional religion of the early Maroons," and observes that the Maroon ancestoral cult developed from the contact of a variety of African cultures. He goes on to say:

> In traditional maroon belief, there is one supreme deity, the omnipotent creator, known as *Yankipong* or *Tata Nyame*, who inhabits the sky....Below *Yankipong* are the spirits of the ancestors ... [and that] ... close contact is maintained between living Maroons and the ancestral spirits .... Under the upper echelon of ancient spirits lies a large body of ancestral spirits whose powers decrease in proportion to their closeness to the living.[168]

Communication between the living and the dead was maintained in traditional ceremony, known as the Kromanti dance (or Kromanti Play), which encompassed dance, music, and language. The actual transmission of prayer was conducted through the medium of the spirit possession (or obeah) of the fete-man or woman. Bilby points to the important place in the ritual of music and dance, fire, drums, "blowing rum" and, if animal sacrifice is involved, of a fowl, especially a white one, and of "Kromanti," the language derived from that of their earliest African ancestors and considered as the tongue of the "first time" Maroons.

While Bilby's study was based on the Maroons who remained in Jamaica, and especially the Windward communities, it would appear to reflect the traditions and rites of the Trelawny Town Maroons as well. In addition, Bilby points to another factor that might have contributed to confounding the efforts of Lieutenant-Governor Wentworth and Reverend Gray. There was, he states, "among the Maroons, a strong ethic of secrecy ...[that] pervades all matters pertaining to traditional ritual." Bilby emphasizes:

> On a more general level, secrecy about traditional Maroon beliefs and practices is a dominant theme running through Maroon culture ... There are supernatural sanctions against the giving out of Maroon knowledge to outsiders, and thus Maroons have developed patterned ways of 'dodging' the queries of meddlesome outsiders ... Those who violate this rule and talk too freely to outsiders are likely to incur the wrath of the ancestors and may suffer some spirit-caused misfortune, such as an illness.[169]

These were obviously strong beliefs and it is perhaps little wonder that Gray's efforts did not lead to whole-scale conversion.[170] In Nova Scotia the religion of the Maroons was remembered with somewhat less analysis. Thomas H. Raddall wrote:

> The worship of Accompang [sic] involved mysterious rites for the good of their souls, and in turn Accompang indulged them in all sorts of orgies for the pleasure of their

flesh. For four years the nocturnal forest about Preston rang with their voodoo chants and orgiastic laughter, and the townsfolk of Halifax and Dartmouth heard dreadful whispers of the rites.[171]

Gray's influence on the religion of the Maroons is hard to measure. When the "old chief Montague, whom all the Maroons honoured, was asked if he had understood the sermon, ... he replied: 'Massa parson say, no mus tief, no mus meddle with somebody wife, no mus quarrel, mus set down softly." It seems that the message of religion was grasped even if it was "in a language not understood."[172] When it was later charged that the Maroons only attended Church in order to get rum, Superintendent Alexander Howe admitted that it was the custom to give them rum at Christmas. However, he explained:

> "[I] would impress upon them that this was not a day for excesses but to every four who went to church ... he would give a bottle of rum the following day. When this, the Captain indignantly offered, is contrasted with the practice 'previously followed' [before he took charge of the Maroons' management] of selecting Sundays and other 'Halowday', for the express purpose of gaming, cock-fighting and debauchery, he did not need to be ashamed of the comparison.[173]

After the establishment of the second Maroon settlement at Boydville, situated on the Great Western highway to Windsor, Wentworth extended Gray's ministry to them as well, explaining that "they have requested the Chaplain to administer public worship among them and he has commenced for one-third of the Sundays — The first day they all attended with decency and attention — brought thirteen of their children who were received to Baptism — and they expressed solicitude for Mr. Gray's return on the Sunday appointed, which will be complied with and continued."[174] The S.P.G continued to help support

Reverend Gray, and "sent him some Bibles, Prayer Books and Religious Tracts for the use of the Maroons, and the neighbouring English congregation to which he also administered."[175]

While the Maroon Town (Preston) residents maintained their old ways, which Arthur Silver characterized as "clinging to their heathenish Coromantee ceremonies and degrading Obeah superstitions,"[176] Wentworth had greater hopes for those at Boydville. In 1799 he wrote:

> These People are sober, industrious — constant in their attendance on public worship, which Mr. Gray administers every third Sunday, to these Maroons and more than one hundred white people, who were before destitute. The Service is performed in one of the Maroon Barns — And has already impressed both descriptions — That they agreed to build a decent Church — and the timber is already on the spot, and a liberal subscription made toward making it useful as soon as possible — In which the Maroons are interested in proportion to their numbers and express great satisfaction therein.[177]

However, other than the baptism of their children, even within the community of Christian converts at Boydville, there is no evidence of the solemnization of marriage or of burial by other than traditional Maroon rites.

Reverend Gray, who had "baptized fifty-five in fourteen months, twenty-six being adults,"[178] was the individual most directly involved in and concerned with the Christianization of the Maroons and he understood their reluctance to alter their traditions. Indeed, "surprisingly, Gray does not seem to display the usual intolerance of other cultures, so prevalent within the North Atlantic World then."[179] In 1798 he admitted to Sir John Wentworth that "on the subject of Marriage and Burial ... the Maroons have certainly admitted neither of these offices," and went on to explain to the Governor:

It is not so easy a thing to eradicate from the mind those attachments, which early habits, and constant practice have endeared to it. They could not be expected all at once to give up to strangers the performance of the last offices to their departed friends.

While Gray allowed that their "tenacity on this" was natural, he nonetheless tried to influence it, although he admitted that the solemnity of the Christian ceremony offered little in exchange for what was "generally the occasion of Festive Excess." Gray also allowed that his efforts likely had, at best, limited success. He wrote:

They bury their dead about their dwellings. I improved this circumstance to represent the dangers of their being thrown up in the course of Tillage — and offered them a part of the Church Yard to their own particular use if they would but consent that I should read the burial Service: it had some Effect upon them but they have not yet called me to the performance of it.

In 1900 Arthur Silver reported that the "sportsman following his game in the autumn woods occasionally stumbles across a few rude heaps of stones which cover their dead."[180]

Gray was equally forthcoming about his influence on Maroon polygamy. While he felt (likely erroneously) that the women were "generally enemies to it" and hoped to "affect the manner of the rising generation," he acknowledged that "the present should carry their customs to the grave." Gray also informed Wentworth that one young man had consented to a Christian marriage but that it had not occurred, writing, "I cannot actually say what was his inducement for declining his Engagement, but suppose that the knowledge of his Intentions produced such discouragement on the part of the Agent [Alexander Ochterlony], that he finally abandoned the Intention."[181]

Wentworth did not blame Gray, whom Wentworth described as

"amicable and conciliating in his Manners, discreet, patient, and ingenious, and peculiarly accomplished for this very laborious and difficult Duty,"[182] for the slow progress of bringing the Maroons to the Church. Both clergyman and schoolmaster met with his approval. In the spring of 1797, when seeking funds from Portland for their work, he praised them: "These Gentlemen," he wrote, "have faithfully and usefully performed their duty, and continue resident therein, not withstanding the apprehensions naturally excited by such a people."[183] Any responsibility for failure he placed at the door of Alexander Ochterlony, the agent who, by February of 1797, was actively engaged in undermining the Lieutenant-Governor's plans for the settlement of the Maroons. In 1799 Wentworth explained:

> Too wisely foreseeing that instruction in Christianity would be attended with peaceful submission, and orderly pursuits he wickedly and for a time but too successfully undermined this best branch of our efforts for their good — by neglecting — despising and dividing public worship — giving rewards for not attending on Sunday — giving feasts — liquor — horse racing and cock fighting on that day — and finding even these temptations did not altogether prevail — he made them believe that the King paid every person that went to church — and that they were cheated by me and the Clergyman of their pay for Sunday — from these and innumerable other such devise — they do not yet attend regularly.[184]

Wentworth made no apology for his initiatives in education and religion. It was a duty incumbent upon him

> to take care that six hundred people of their description should not be settled in a province under his administration, without a careful and faithful establishment for their instruction in the christian religion; and in reading and

writing the english language — by which means alone can any people be reclaimed and fitted for living in a british colony.185

Despite any inroads that the teaching of Christianity might have made, it is likely that the ancient religion, which "taught the Maroons that their god... was responsible for their good fortunes" thus generating their trust and faith in their god's ultimate power, continued to provide a common bond within the Maroon community.[186] It was obviously a force that also separated the Maroons from the larger Nova Scotia community of which they were to be so temporarily a part.

CHAPTER 6

Resistance to Settlement

At the end of 1796, Sir John Wentworth could recount the "progress already made" with some pride. The entire Maroon establishment was in place. Lands and houses had been provided and Commissioner Ochterlony was living in Maroon Hall, which became the centre of Maroon activities.[187] In addition, the school and church with resident staff had been established and Dr. John Oxley, who had accompanied the Maroons from Jamaica, continued to provide them with medical attention.[188] Hovering over this administrative network was Wentworth's guiding hand, fussing over every detail of the project.[189]

Sir John was not, however, blind to the problems of successfully settling the Maroons. He acknowledged "the Difficulties that must be expected to occur in removing [them] to a new country, in changing the Manners of War and Hunting to those of Peace and patient Industry, and in submitting to be considered without Terror, or the Self-importance derived from it."[190] In December the Duke of Portland extended his congratulations "on the success which has attended your endeavours."[191] Wentworth, however, had little opportunity to dwell on congratulations as the Maroon settlement experiment was rife with problems. The dissatisfaction of the Trelawnys due to the weather, self-serving leadership, financial problems and disputes within the Maroon community itself, served to chip away and finally shatter Wentworth's hopes for the Maroon settlement. Even Sir John Wentworth's persistent optimism concerning the establishment of the Maroons in Nova Scotia was strained by the winter of 1796-97.

Despite the concerns expressed by some, the problem was not that the Maroons were more adversely affected by the severity of the weather than was anyone else in the province. Indeed, after suffering poor health due to the months of privation during the war in Jamaica and the subsequent long, uncomfortable voyage to Nova Scotia, the winter saw most of the Maroons more healthy than before. At least this is what Dr. Oxley claimed.[192] The problem was that the Maroons simply did not like the weather and saw no reason why they should put up with it. In Jamaica, while the summit of the Blue Mountains occasionally has a light frost in the winter months, the normal temperature range was from 24° C to 30° C in the day and 18.5° C at night, rarely falling below 15.6° C. The forced change from this temperate climate to the extremes of Nova Scotia could hardly appeal to the Maroons.

While the discomfort of the Maroons was likely increased by their cramped quarters in often drafty log cabins, the winter of 1796-97 was very severe. In 1797 Alexander Howe explained their position:

> The arrival of the Maroons in this country after a long voyage, sickly, driven from the place of their nativity; no preparation for their immediate reception, sudden purchases obliged to be made to procure houses habitable for them, *everything* at first conspired with the longest and severest winter known in this country within the memory of Man to hurt and distress the prospects before them. [193]

The weather-related concerns of the Maroons were soon manifest:

> [E]arly in September, the morning and evening made them feel a degree of cold to which they were strangers, they were not then sufficiently clothed, nor were they well lodged …[After their placement] they at first began with some cheerfulness to cut wood for their winter use; the women and children brought it out of the woods on their heads, and piled it round their houses; but as the season advanced this service was performed with much less alacrity, and a considerable degree of ill humor became visible.[194]

On 29 October 1796 Quarrell noted that "the increasing cold of the weather had made the Maroons, particularly some of the bad subjects, very peevish and discontent."[195]

The severity of the winter was also attested to by Wentworth. On 21 April 1797 he informed Portland, "The Maroons have passed thro', the longest and most rigorous winter known since the first settlement of Halifax, much better than could be expected." Furthermore, Sir John cheerfully explained:

> They have maintained as good health, as any other inhabitants, with less [sic] . . . casualties from frost than I apprehended, arising from their inexperience and reluctant use of shoes and stockings — I do not find that anyone has lost more than a joint of a toe or finger, and but a few of these.[196]

Even the process of "their civilization" was affected by the onslaught of the winter. In 1798 Reverend Gray explained:

> The winter however/ which set in early/ becoming dayly [sic] more tempestuous, our Exercises were occasionally interrupted and such was the degree of cold that, notwithstanding your care to have a stove erected in the church, even the Natives of this country were frequently unable to attend — as the Maroons of course were incapable of encountering this severe weather, I was under the necessity, though with extreme reluctance/of discontinuing a practice which had proved so highly useful; still hoping that the return of warm weather, would enable me to resume it.[197]

On 7 May 1797 Wentworth admitted that the Maroons "have not yet overcome the apprehensions caused by the extreme rigorous and unusual long winter and backward spring, which has only this day given any pleasant warmth — and both together have been near three months longer than has been known since the settlement of Halifax in the year 1749."[198] The severe winter saw snow several feet deep on the ground,[199] and, as late as June 1, it was still "so wet and cold that the labour of planting our potatoes at Maroon Hall is thrown away."[200] These conditions were indeed a shock to the 532 Maroons who managed to survive the winter.[201] Seeking a solution, in April 1797 they had secretly petitioned General Walpole for "relief from our present miserable situation."[202] They asked to be moved "to some warmer climate," and to be relieved "from those sufferings ... which in this country we see no end."[203] Obviously missing the comfort of their "delectable mountains in Jamaica ... Montague [James] again led the resistance movement .... In this case it was against climate and it was conducted not on the battlefield but in the diplomatic/political arena."[204]

Colonel Montague James, a title he was granted in Nova Scotia, continued to be recognized as the leader of the Maroons by the colonial officials and likely by the majority of the Maroons themselves. George Ross portrayed him as a "wise, judicious, humane and even-tempered leader," who governed by consideration and discussion. After the Maroons left Nova Scotia he retained and entrenched his position of leadership with his people.

Not all Nova Scotians, despite shared problems in acquiring sufficient fuel and provisions, were equally inconvenienced by the winter weather:

> The officers and gentry and their ladies indulged in lively sleigh drives along the Windsor road on sunny afternoons ... [and] ... skating was a popular pastime. Crowds went to the Northwest Arm, where 'judges, lawyers, high officials, rectors, curates, and the dignified Bishop Inglis himself joined hands with the crowd. Colonels, mayors, captains, middies were all on skates, and the fair sex were out in full force'.[205]

Needless to say, the Maroons were neither involved nor impressed.

In fact, "after a very few cold nights, they had cried out that it was impossible for them ever to exist in such a climate, and they earnestly begged to be removed to one more mild."[206] The Maroons so remembered the cold that three years later, in Sierra Leone, they informed Governor Ludlam that "the country they had left had been too cold for them — that made them leave it."[207] Indeed, their then Superintendent, George Ross, noted in his Journal on 17 October 1800:

> The General [sic] (Montague James) complains much of the heat — but the remembrance of the cold of Nova Scotia will ever be a sufficient check. The Maroons would, I believe, grumble not a little on account of the heat were this their first country after Jamaica.[208]

CHAPTER 7

The Maroon Establishment: Disagreement and Intrigue

One of the most disruptive forces ranged against the successful settlement of the Maroons was the disagreement among the three principal administrators of their establishment — Lieutenant-Governor Sir John Wentworth; William Dawes Quarrell, their Jamaican-appointed Commissary General; and his assistant, Alexander Ochterlony. Wentworth's intention was to settle the Maroons together in a defined community. Quarrell, who at first seemed to support this idea, ultimately wished to integrate them into Nova Scotia by breaking up the Maroon community, while Ochterlony, with plans of his own, worked secretly to undermine any effort to settle the Maroons in Nova Scotia. Each had their allies and detractors among the local citizens and military personnel. The Maroons, however, were not simply pawns in this contest of influence and will. They were able and willing, individually and collectively, to take full advantage of the situation to effect their own purposes.

The division of purpose that developed among the officials of the Maroon establishment was not initially apparent. Indeed, Wentworth's early impressions of the representatives of the Jamaican government were positive. For example, in his 20 September 1796 report to Portland he commented on the "judicious choice of Mr. Quarrell and Mr. Ochterlony to accompany and superintend the interests of these poor People," and on "the affectionate zeal, unvaried assiduity, great judgement and perfect dis-interestedness which these Gentlemen invariably exert."[209] Similarly, in October, Wentworth commended the "zeal, patience and affectionate care" of both Quarrell and Ochterlony and lauded their "infinite merit in conducting the difficult and important trust committed to them."[210] In December 1796 Portland had asked Wentworth to "be so good as to acquaint Mr. Commissary Quarrel [sic] that the manner in which he has fulfilled his commission has not escaped His Majesty's notice," and, consequently, on Balcarres' suggestion, Quarrell was appointed "to be of the Council of His Island of Jamaica."[211] Wentworth, in turn, reported that Quarrell "received his appointment to the Jamaica Council as a reward for his conduct to the Maroons, 'with the highest sense of dutiful gratitude, zeal and loyalty to His Majesty'."[212] Unfortunately, his good opinion was to be badly shaken before the spring of 1797, and by June 1799 Wentworth charged that "Mr. Quarrell and his assistant, conceiving different selfish views, secretly counteracted each other's measures,"[213] and caused the failure of the settlement of the Maroons.

Because the winter of 1796-97 was very severe, "the want of provisions was felt, and the scarcity of flour threatened a famine in the town,"[214] just as it had in the winter of 1795. To alleviate the distress, Quarrell sailed for New York on 23 February 1797, returning a month later with flour and other provisions.[215] After this trip to New York and Philadelphia,[216] Quarrell took up residence in Dartmouth[217] and left Ochterlony to live in Maroon Hall at the heart of the Maroon community. This circumstance allowed Ochterlony every opportunity to develop and pursue his own aims. Moreover, despite Wentworth's regular visits to the Maroons[218] in the summer and fall of 1796, he apparently failed to note that, as the winter progressed, the Maroons were increasingly susceptible to the plans formulated by Alexander Ochterlony.

Dr. Oxley later reported, "In the month of February I found Mr. Ochterlony was forming several plans for counteracting Mr. Quarrell's intentions of settling the Maroons in this province (though not openly declared),"[219] knowledge of which Wentworth was "too long uninformed."[220] Ochterlony, as reported by Benjamin Gerrish Gray, had "before the expiration of the first winter ... altered his mind about settling the Maroons, and instead of giving his sincere support to the plan he had himself been instrumental in forming, he made use of his situation secretly to frustrate its completion, and determined to carry the Maroons from this country."[221]

Ochterlony's campaign to undermine the settlement plans of Wentworth and Quarrell found fertile ground in the Maroons' winter of discontent. While they

> prepared to pass with gloomy resignation a long and comfortless winter, it was an exertion to which at times they were not equal, to leave their stoves, and assemble at each others houses to deliberate upon their present miserable situation, but such meetings were sometimes held and their resolutions had uniformly but one object, their removal to a warmer country. Jamaica if possible, but anywhere rather than remain in Nova-Scotia.[222]

Ochterlony reminded them of the warm climate they had left behind "as nothing short of a Paradise, the abundance and delicacy of its fruits, enumerated and dwelt upon, till their mouths were watering." Nova Scotia, on the other hand,

> was daily spoken of before them, as Cold, barron, fit only for bears and moose to live in, or to use a little of his eloquence, 'The Devils own Country, A Hell of a Country, A Country fit only for the Devil to remain in'... [while] the Inhabitants of the Country, they were said to be, a Set of Rogues, a pack of Rascals, the greatest villains upon earth, ... a parcel of thieves and pick pockets.[223]

In response to the question raised at his table, "Oh what one might do, with these fellows, if he had them wholly to himself," Ochterlony, "upheld by the wicked machinations of his friends and coadjutors," revealed "to them his design of removing them from this, to some warm country, more congenial to their constitutions, and habits. And they were given to understand that their friend General Walpole, was assisting to get this business established." From veiled hints to bold assertions, "Mr. Ochterlony began to hold meetings of their Captains and principal men, on purpose to consider the matter and to consult and advise with one another, how to act in it."[224] James Moody reported that he had heard Ochterlony declare "with heat and vehemence" against "any projected Maroon settlement in Nova Scotia." Ochterlony "denounced any Maroon 'fools' who would work when Jamaica 'had their possessions', and if Wentworth tried to force the Maroons to work, then they would have 'spirit enough to stab him in the midst of his garrison.'"[225]

Brave plans were hatched wherein the Maroons, with Ochterlony as their colonel and leader, would conquer Guadalope, St. Domingo, Cuba, Hispaniola, or some other enemy coast. Yet another scheme was to "purchase the ship Elizabeth and take them to the Cape of Good Hope"[226] or India, with the Maroons "saying just put arms in our hands and land us anywhere in a warm climate & we will make settlements and room for ourselves."[227] Yet another scheme of "Mischievous Machinations" was the proposed migration "of the Maroons to Georgia, as if the United States would be willing to accept a … dangerous people."[228] At one of the meetings, it was reported that "a Bible was called for, and … the Maroons entered into Solomn Engagements to adhere to, and be guided by Mr. Ochterlony, and that he swore to stand by them, and procure their removal."[229]

Ochterlony's purpose in this campaign can only be assumed. On the one hand he might have been genuinely moved by "affectionate zeal and infinite merit" to secure the best interests of the Maroons. On the other hand his motives might have been more personal. The latter is what some of his contemporaries believed. Reverend Gray questioned "whether it arose from a desire of ingratiating himself with his charge, for it was notorious that very strong prejudices existed against him,[230] or whether from the ambition of having the entire conduct of them in another country."[231] Others were more unequivocal. Theophilus Chamberlain's comment — "And who so likely, to be made Governor, of this new colony of Maroons, as their victorious colonel?" — reflected the views of many on Ochterlony's personal ambition. Wentworth attributed the source of the disaffection of the Maroons to "Persons evidently desirous of getting Possession of these poor People for the Sake of the Means afforded for their Support and Settlement,"[232] a charge he likely would not confine to Ochterlony but extend to some provincial land owners as well.[233]

A strategy soon emerged in the Ochterlony camp to bring about the removal of the Maroons. Chamberlain piously intoned:

> The mischievously minded, are seldom long without some ingenious device, a deep laid scheme began in a short time to make its appearance. What, said a friend of Mr. Ochterlony, would you do with the Maroons, should they refuse to work here, and persevere in it. And sure enough, within a very few days, they all as one man, laid down their axes and refused to strike a blow more ... acting on a regular system.[234]

While the Maroons refused to work, complaining of illness, of the cold, and of physical intimidation, concerns were being raised over the state of affairs at Maroon Hall, where Ochterlony and his friends held court. Gray charged that "the progress towards depravity was rapid indeed. Maroon Hall was the very fountain of Wantonness" and that Ochterlony and his cronies had "proved their sincere attachment to their [the Maroons] welfare by promoting the prostitution of their females and encouraging their vicious inclinations to inhuman sports and riot."[235] While others complained of cock fighting, card playing, and drinking, Theophilus Chamberlain's charges against Ochterlony were more specific. He wrote:

> It was well known that he kept, five or six, and often more, of the finest Maroon girls, constantly in his house, and several in his bed chamber, and that this seraglio was kept, not merely for himself, but for the convenience of his devout and religious friends and assistants in the projected removal of the Maroons.[236]

Alexander Howe also condemned Ochterlony, but perhaps on other than strictly moral grounds, as he pointed that the "entertainment" was "at a constant (extra) expense to the Establishment."[237] Immorality was not a charge levied by Sir John who, according to local tradition, later had a Maroon mistress, his wife, Lady Frances, "being so often in the arms of another."[238] Moreover in April 1797, the first secret Maroon petition had been sent to the British Parliament, by way of General Walpole, over the mark of Montague James.[239] While undoubtedly written with the concurrence of Ochterlony (and perhaps with the knowledge of Quarrell), Wentworth was apparently ignorant of its existence until the spring of 1798.

Such a situation could not be tolerated for long. When Ochterlony's actions became as "apparent as the noon day sun ... those about him thought themselves justifiable in representing his conduct to Mr. Quarrell." The Superintendent, who was not convinced of the block settlement of the Maroons but had agreed to their removal to Nova Scotia, tried to curb the actions of his subordinate. In May he informed Wentworth of the problem and, after united admonition, Ochterlony "promised to reform."[240] The damage, however, was done. Awaking to the situation, Wentworth moved to limit the effect in late May 1797.[241] He met with the Maroons and entered into an agreement with them,

> that on condition they would be quiet and obedient, make what improvements on their places they could, and fairly try this country for one year, if in the end of it, they should still say that they could not be contented in this country, your Excellency would then write to know whether it would consist with His Majesty's pleasure, that they should be removed to any other place.[242]

On 28 May 1797 Wentworth's written commitment was addressed to "Colonel Montague James and Captain Smith, on behalf of and for the Maroons now residing at Preston, in the Province of Nova Scotia," which he felt had bound them to "this Day Twelvemonth, viz. on the

28th day of May in the year 1798."[243] To Portland, Wentworth confided that he had "convinced them of the wisdom of trying another year, when their wish might be more reasonable and merit more consideration." Ever confident, the Lieutenant-Governor added, "I do not find any just cause to alter my former sentiments and expectations respecting their residence in this country."[244]

While Wentworth was sure that the Maroons "unanimously approved" of the trial year, others were not so certain. Chamberlain asserted that "all the subtilty of the Serpent described by Milton was practiced upon the poor Maroons," and whispers about Wentworth's intent and honesty and questions, such as why not move us now rather than wait a year, were posed.[245] For some the proposal had become a promise,[246] and Ochterlony and his confederates were detected to be once again interfering with the plan to settle the Maroons. As late as 2 June 1797 Wentworth was hopeful that Ochterlony had reformed. In fact, on being informed of Commissioner Quarrell's impending resignation, Wentworth

> conferred with Mr. Ouchterlong [sic], who was Deputy Commissary, and has Qualifications to be useful; who consents to remain with them, and faithfully and cordially to use his utmost Endeavours to do away any improper Ideas that may have arisen, and to carry my Directions into Effect; in which Case I may represent his Services, with a just Hope that they will be graciously considered.[247]

Wentworth's hopes were again disappointed and in July he advised Portland that "other Views and Objectives having been evidently entertained since Christmas last by Mr. Ouchterlong [sic], has in some measure retarded the progress that might otherwise be obtained, and which we concur in opinion will proceed better when Mr. Ouchterlong [sic] is removed from them."[248] In a letter to Governor Balcarres, dated 4 August 1797, Wentworth complained:

Petitions to the King, privately, and insidiously concealed from me, were prepared, and under the direction of Mr. Ochterlony sent home. Gentlemen of the Army and Navy, and passengers going to England, [were] invited to the Settlement to hear these poor people utter discontents, which were taught them.[249]

He also complained of Ochterlony's failure to conform to the instructions of his superiors. Instead of reform, "every discouragement, and opposition daily increased, notoriously from the same source, and to a degree that required my positive and immediate interference." Finally, with the support of Quarrell, Wentworth demanded "the removal of Mr. Ochterlony from all concern or intercourse with the business."[250] Wentworth's later memory of Ochterlony's conduct was that within ten days the Deputy had "departed from his promise," and instead he used his position "to poison the minds of the Maroons." This, however, was not the limit of his misconduct. As Balcarres explained, Ochterlony's actions tended

to stir up sedition among the inhabitants. Mr. Quarrell represented his conduct in the strongest terms; and insisted upon the necessity of immediately separating him from the Maroons. As he was dangerous to all peace and order, Sir John Wentworth could no longer palliate, or place any hopes of a better conduct. It was evident he had formed a party; and was pursuing with them a system ruinous to the settlement, and leading to disseminate sedition; for which purpose the grossest language, falsehoods, and indecencies were outrageously scattered abroad. Sir John Wentworth of course approved of Mr. Quarrell's sentiments; and he (Mr. Quarrell) accordingly dismissed Mr. Ochterlony.[251]

On 12 August 1797 Wentworth informed Portland that Ochterlony, who "took temporary employment with Dr. Bray's Associates"[252] and

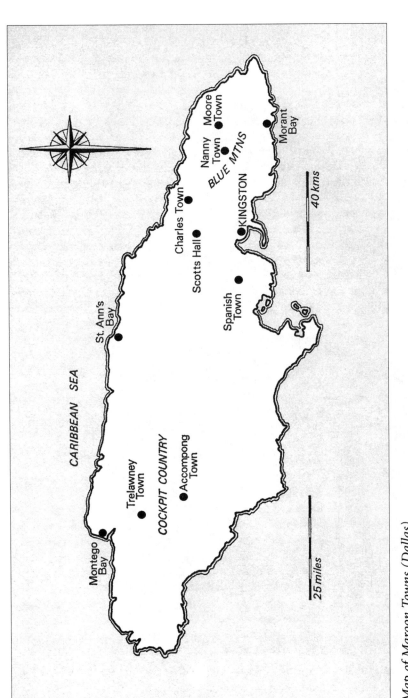

Map of Maroon Towns (Dallas)

View of Port Royal and Kingston Harbour with ship firing salute in foreground. (Long, History of Jamaica v.2)

Engraving of Old Cudjoe meeting the British for the purposes of making a peace accord. (Dallas)

The Earl of Balcarres,
Governor of Jamaica at the
time of the Second Maroon
War.

A Spanish chasseur from Cuba with a dog, similar to those which were
brought to Jamaica to chase the Maroons out of the hills. (Dallas)

Trelawny Town under attack from British cavalry. (Robinson)

Sir John Wentworth, Lieutenant-Governor of Nova Scotia. (Hood Museum, Dartmouth, NH)

Prince Edward, 1798. (Communications NS)

Portrait of Leonard Parkinson with musket and cutlass. (Robinson)

View of Maroons in ambush in Jamaica. (Robinson)

Woolford sketch of Reverend Gray's parsonage. (Nova Scotia Museum)

Painting of HMS Asia *at Halifax, ca. 1800. (Maritime Museum of the Atlantic)*

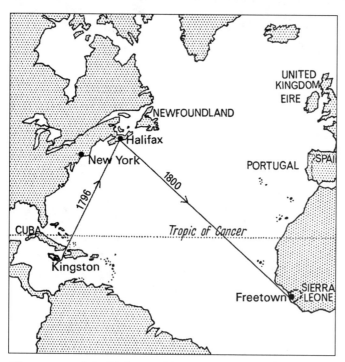

The voyage of the Trelawny Town Maroons. (Robinson)

had been seeking employment in Jamaica, "in a few days departs from this country."[253] While his departure date is not confirmed, Ochterlony was in Boston on 7 December 1797 on his way home to Savanna La Mar, Jamaica.[254] In 1798 he "defended himself at large on oath before the House of Assembly in Jamaica, denying or justifying, the charges that were made against him" by Wentworth. The Assembly of Jamaica "fully acquitted him, and also granted him a renumeration for his services."[255] In Nova Scotia he is remembered to the present-day by the Dartmouth street named after him.[256] While "the inquietude [that] existed during the latter time Mr. Ochterlony superintended them"[257] did not end with his dismissal, it must not be supposed that all of the Maroons favoured Ochterlony's ongoing efforts to undermine the Nova Scotia experiment. Some, especially those who established the community at Boydville, apparently did not.

Wentworth, again with Quarrell's reported approval, appointed Captain Alexander Howe (1749-1813) to take charge of Ochterlony's responsibilities and he took up residence in Maroon Hall. Howe's military career had begun when he was 13 or 14 years of age. He served in North America, England, Ireland, and for many years in Jamaica. In 1783 he had sold his commission and returned to Nova Scotia to farm in Granville, close to his birthplace of Annapolis Royal. He soon became involved in politics and, despite the split between the loyalists and his own pre-loyalist connections, he was elected (albeit with political dispute) in 1786 to the Assembly, where he remained until 1799. He also held the offices of justice of the peace, judge of the Inferior Court of Common Pleas for Annapolis County, and collector of taxes and excise duties for the county. In 1791 he had recruited among the black loyalists for the migration to Sierra Leone. His military career resumed in 1793 when he became Captain of a company in Wentworth's newly raised Royal Nova Scotia Regiment.[258]

Howe was already part of the "Maroon Establishment" and, because Prince Edward saw him as "so usefully employed with the command of the Maroons," other officers instead of Howe were detailed to the Cape Breton station.[259] Wentworth later explained to Portland, perhaps to hush any questioning of the elevation of Howe, that "Lieutenant General His Royal Highness Prince Edward … arranged Captain Howe's Regimental Duty into that precinct, at my request, as he is peculiarly qualified for that Service, and is aided by his Military Authority."[260] Quarrell, meanwhile, "directed Mr. Chamberlain to call the Maroons out to work. . . . The words he put in my mouth to make use of on the occasion were 'No work, No Yam'."[261]

Fears that the Maroons might break into the stores and kill their cattle for food rather than return to work, as had been threatened, proved unfounded as they soon returned to their labours. Whether this response was due to the threat of withholding provisions, the change in the superintendent, the appearance of a company of soldiers from the Royal Nova Scotia Regiment, or simply the improvement in the weather, is difficult to determine. The effort, however, to create farmers of war-riors was further stymied, according to Bryan Edwards, by the Maroon tradition in Jamaica, that "the labours of the field … such as they were, (as well as every other species of drudgery), were performed by the women."[262] This relatively rare comment on the life and role of Maroon women in the records was supported by Wentworth who also noted that the "women are accustomed to work, full as much as the men, who take care to require it."[263] Perhaps the advantage of this labour in polygamy explains, if only in part, why Maroon men "part with their interest in their wives" only if compensation were made.[264]

These actions and reactions around the Maroons could not escape the notice or concern of the local population. On 28 June 1797 the Assembly passed a resolution requesting the Lieutenant-Governor "to inform the House on what Terms and conditions a certain Description of Black Persons, known by the Appelation of Maroons" came to Nova Scotia, who was to provide for them, and what measures had been taken to prevent them "from eventually becoming chargeable to the County of Halifax."[265] On 29 June 1797 Wentworth assured the Assembly that the Maroons "have behaved orderly, peaceably and quietly since their arrival" and that their budget was "totally and entirely independent of this Province, which will not be encumbered with any cost or charge for these people."[266] With this the Assembly had to be content, but a year later Wentworth remembered their concerns when he reminded Jamaica that the Maroons' settlement "is acceded to by the people, rather than desirable, and no means invited."[267]

On 22 July 1797 Commissary General William Quarrell tendered his resignation in favour of Wentworth. Wentworth, however, "prevailed on Mr. Quarrell to postpone his intended voyage to Jamaica for sometime, and to continue his good offices among these people, which he has benevolently consented to, as he is humanely interested for the welfare and happy settlement of the Maroons, in this Province."[268] Indeed, Quarrell did not completely control his own itinerary. In November 1797 Wentworth again complained to Portland that the financial arrangements that Jamaica had set up to support the Maroons had not been "effectual" and that "Mr. Quarrell feels himself much injured by the Dishonour to his Bills." Jamaica's "Refusal of his Drafts" caused Halifax merchants to suspend his credit and Quarrell "could not obtain any Money, or Supplies … nor would any person take his Bills on any terms." As a consequence of these financial concerns, "The Bill-holders decline consenting to his Return to Jamaica."[269]

These financial complications brought Wentworth into direct conflict with the Duke of Portland. In the spring of 1797 the "bills drawn on Maroon accounts by their agents, were not being honoured and Wentworth, rather unwisely, endorsed them himself. This brought down the full weight of the parsimonious Portland on him and Wentworth was made to see his error in no uncertain terms."[270]

Eventually Quarrell, after being "detained in Nova Scotia and other parts of America, fifteen months after his mission was considered at an end," took advantage of "the relief afforded by Messrs. Cochrane," to whom Quarrell paid £1000 "by way of profit to them," for settling the dishonoured bills. This, Quarrell explained, "satisfactorily settled the business for me, and thereby released me from a further detention in Halifax, where I had already been detained so long, to the manifest injury if my own private affairs."[271]

While Quarrell remained in Nova Scotia until 29 April 1798,[272] and while Wentworth commended his conduct to Balcarres,[273] his ongoing role was not merely supportive. He was likely more than, as Dallas suggests, "a spectator of the state of the Maroon settlement."[274] On 8 August 1797, apparently still unconvinced about the mode of settlement of the Maroons, he wrote Alexander Howe, who was "well known and highly preferred by Quarrell,"[275] and complimented him on "taking upon yourself an office which I do not flatter you in saying there is no man here fit for but yourself."

Quarrell asked Howe if he believed that the Maroons could indeed be settled in Nova Scotia, how they might be affected by the climate, if they would work, if encouraged, and why the early effort had not been more successful.[276] Responding immediately, Howe acknowledged Quarrell's "good opinion" and confided that he had "reason to think I possess a considerable portion of the confidence, and regard of the Maroons." He further stated that he believed that the Maroons could indeed be settled in Nova Scotia but acknowledged, "It will take considerable time before all their necessary wants can be supplied from their own labour however Prolific the Soil." Pointing to the example of the remaining black loyalists, "well settled and living at their ease" after only thirteen years in residence, he suggested that the "whole management of them with other causes" was what led to the migration of so many of them. The climate, he opined, would be tolerable except for the three coldest months which they could survive "by warm houses and large fires." The Maroons would certainly work, he asserted, if encouraged, and "a proof is that I have on application given passes to a great many who have engaged themselves to labour for several Gentlemen at Halifax by the week and by the month, many are employed about the County and get high wages for clearing land, making hay, driving carts, and various other labours." He also boasted, "I find no difficulty to get as many Maroons to labour as I want at very low wages to make bricks, dig Cellars, carry stones, hoe potatoes, make hay or do anything I direct them to do," and praised the industry of the women, boys, and girls in gathering berries, etc., to sell at the Halifax market. Finally, while wording his charges carefully, he left little doubt that the author of the Maroons' discontent was Ochterlony, noting "that much discouragement was thrown on their exertions by knowing that Mr. Ochterlony did not wish them to work."[277]

Quarrell, it seems, was not convinced. He apparently believed that, in Jamaica, the agreement "which kept the bodies of Maroons as a distinct tribe in the strongest parts of the country, instead of their being merged in the general negro population ...was the cause of all the subsequent trouble," — trouble that Quarrell feared would develop in Nova Scotia as well.[278] On his departure from Nova Scotia the Maroons sent Quarrell an address which, according to Dallas, caught up to him in Boston, thanking him for his attention, the "very friendly asylum" of his house in Dartmouth, and asking that he intervene on their behalf with the House of Assembly in Jamaica with their request to "be removed to some other country more congenial to people of their complexion." Quarrell, who had already expressed his opinion on the Maroon settlement in Nova Scotia in a letter to a member of the Jamaican Assembly, was delayed in New York "in consequence of the depredations of the French cruizers [sic]"and did not arrive in Jamaica until the end of October.[279] The Jamaican government appreciated his representation on their behalf and he "was voted the sum of £5,000 by the Jamaican Assembly for meritorious services and to compensate him for expenses and sufferings."[280]

Wentworth boasted to Balcarres: "Since Captain Howe has Superintended the whole settlement wears a new and promising appearance, the people are all cheerfully at work, there is good humor returning, some have solicited to be settled for life, and they gradually abandon all the plans foolishly and wickedly made."[281]

But he could ill afford any comfort with the situation. He had been advised by Quarrell that the government of Jamaica had decided to limit further assistance to the Maroons to "ten pounds each person." In August 1797 he objected forcefully to Balcarres asserting, "I am certain it is inadequate to the purpose intended however prudently and wisely applied," and pointed out that Jamaica must bear the cost for their mistake in appointing Ochterlony to his position. The Duke of Portland supported Wentworth in his argument that "the Expense which may be incurred on their Account until such Time as they are able to provide for themselves ... the amount of it must be defrayed by the Island of Jamaica, conformably to the Intention, originally expressed by its Legislature at the Time the Maroons were sent to Nova Scotia."[282]

However, Portland was generally much more likely to chide Wentworth about Jamaica's failure to pay its bills than he was to suggest how to force or help Jamaica meet its responsibilities. Indeed, the Jamaican House of Assembly rejected Wentworth's appeals and apparently ignored or explained away Portland's. They argued that the Island had never committed itself to "permanent support" of the Maroons of Trelawny Town; that Nova Scotia was not their choice of settlement; that they had already expended £41,000 currency; and that the Maroons were "atrocious delinquents" exiled for rebellion and not colonizers. They promised that Jamaica would grant another £6,000 sterling for the year ending 22 July 1798, but thereafter it would not "make any other grants for the future support of the Maroons."[283]

A letter published in the *Columbian Centinel*, a Boston newspaper, dated July 1797 but printed on 16 December 1797, and no doubt designed to embarrass Governor Wentworth, contained the case for the removal of the Maroons. Signed 'Humanitus', it warned that the Maroons would "remain a burden upon the public, during a period beyond calculation; and should *Britain* or *Jamaica* at any time, withhold their support, the *Maroons* must either become dependants on the country of *Nova Scotia*, or maintain their families by plunder." Obviously supporting the anti-settlement faction, 'Humanitus' went on to write: "[W]hen the great and continued expense, or the fatal consequences of their despair shall at length point out that the expediency of their removal, perhaps that measure may finally be adopted, which both policy and humanity now cries so loudly should not be delayed."[284]

Whether written by Ochterlony or one of his supporters (or perhaps even by Quarrell), the letter, which appealed to the worst fears of the local population (violence and increased taxes), and to the humanity of assenting to the migration of the Maroons, likely provided additional problems for Wentworth and more ammunition to his enemies.

Adding to Wentworth's discomfort, William Cottnam Tonge, a provincial landowner, Naval Officer, Member of the Assembly, leader of the "Country Party," and Wentworth's political opponent, had approached the Lieutenant-Governor with an alternative plan to settle the Maroons. Tonge, who perhaps represented the general opinion of landowners in need of workers, "proposed to take three hundred at ten pounds per head." As Wentworth explained, Tonge had prefaced this proposal with the observation that his Estate was in debt, but claimed this speculation would help ease that circumstance, which Wentworth thought might be so. However, he could not help asking, "How then was it [Tonge's proposal] to be applied to the support of the Maroons?" Wentworth believed that "the Maroons would not go with him [Tonge] unless compelled by military force." He was supported in this contention by Reverend Gray.[285] Wentworth added, "Nor would the Inhabitants of the Township receive them, with less coercion, which would have been as unjust, as unwise to insist upon."[286] Later, in further explanation, Wentworth wrote:

> The sending such a description of people among the inhabitants who ... had conceived aversions and abhorrence to their character, would certainly have occasioned very great uneasiness and discontent, if not more serious consequences; and the Lieutenant-Governor could not have justified himself to His Majesty, for permitting a people so lately in arms against his government and authority, and still complaining of injustice and ill treatment to be located at a distance from the garrison of Halifax — an invitation to the emissaries of France, and every other enemy to order and good government.[287]

In any event, there is little doubt that Wentworth took some pleasure in informing Tonge, whom he saw as a part of the anti-settlement intrigue, that "as a plan for the settlement of these people has already been arranged, and in considerable progress, I cannot enter into any other."[288]

While this refusal might have provided Wentworth with some personal satisfaction (as did the information that Tonge's estate had been "put up to sale at public auction"), it did little to solve his ongoing problem with the attitude of the Maroon Town residents. Despite the promise of a year's grace, a number of Maroon petitions were received by the British authorities, again unknown to Wentworth, during the summer and fall of 1797, from James and others concerning and concerned with the Maroons.[289] In March 1798 Wentworth finally received copies of the petitions and on 23 June 1798 he submitted his response to all the charges they contained.

Principal among the accusations was a letter (which Robin Winks suggests was written by Quarrell himself) charging Wentworth with maintaining an expensive "Establishment" which plundered the Jamaican government; with misrepresenting the success of the Maroon experiment; and, among other thrusts, accusing him of personally profiting from the management of the Maroon affairs. Wentworth responded with indignation, protesting that he had "acted in all this business from the most disinterested and purest motives and duty to the King, and justice to the island of Jamaica." He pointed out that the "Establishment" had been created by Quarrell and Ochterlony and that his only error was in reporting a Christian marriage within the Maroon community.

Included in this response from Wentworth were letters from "Several of the Gentlemen employed … on the subject of their conduct and the complaints against the management of this service."[290] These testimonials — from Howe, Hartshorne, Tremaine, Oxley, Moody, Gray, and Chamberlain — while sometimes appearing self-serving, were solidly supportive of the Lieutenant-Governor. Howe's comment on the anonymous charges was that "my surprise is far less than my indignation."[291] Chamberlain, ever more verbose, railed against

Anonymous letters, others under fictitious names, petitions signed with Maroon marks witnessed by Apprentice boys, and others with names signed of Maroons who cannot write, and not witnessed at all, are surely modes of address, suited only for the Assassins of France, who thrive by nothing but fraud and inequity.[292]

Uniformly they blamed Ochterlony and his friends for the troubles, protested their honesty, and declared, like Wentworth, the purity of their purpose. The statement of a merchant of such noted honesty as Lawrence Hartshorne, "one of the favoured recipients of official patronage,"[293] about the price of flour was easily accepted by the British authorities. Furthermore:

John Oxley, whom Lord Balcarres himself had appointed surgeon to the Maroons, submitted an unqualified statement of support for the Governor. Nor did he back Quarrell in his contention that the Maroons should have been dispersed throughout the colony, for this would have broken down family ties, removed the Negroes from their one market, Halifax, and taken those who had received land around Boydville away from their only basis for stability. In any case, Wentworth had brought the more refractory Maroons down from Preston to Bedford Basin in the spring, so there now were three settlements, and any further fragmentation would be foolish.[294]

Reverend Gray also opposed any further fragmentation of the community:

But what [he asked] must become of the chances of their reform, when their Instruction, / hardly making impression when collected, and its force directed to a single point / is dispersed in several directions — If they were separated, the

Island of Jamaica must keep a teacher for Every family, or every assemblage of them, or all hope of their Conversion must be abandoned.[295]

Wentworth, responding later to Quarrell's charge that he sought charge of the Maroons and, at least by implication, Jamaican largesse, declared that he had "never conceived such a desire (regard to his own ease & interest might have caused the reverse, but would not admit of such a wish) nor did he ever express or write a sentence, or take any one step or measure to that end, or with that view."[296] Portland accepted Wentworth's explanations but "encouraged Jamaica to send out an agent to take charge of the Maroon's finances." While he also refused, in his official position, to accept any more Maroon petitions, "even one so engagingly phrased as that of January, which protested that they could never 'thrive where the Pine Apple does not' — he nonetheless asked Wentworth to answer each of their complaints, and those of Quarrell who no longer was writing anonymously, as they were raised."[297]

William Cottnam Tonge and Captain John Hale were two of Ochterlony's friends who Wentworth identified as part of the anti-settlement intrigue. They were also two of the many officers whom Prince Edward recommended for promotion. In July 1797 Edward Augustus informed Wentworth that he wanted Tonge "to be appointed to the Command of the 2nd Battalion" that the Prince proposed to add to the provincial militia. Earlier, in April 1797, he had reminded his older and higher-ranking brother, Prince Frederick, the Duke of York and Albany, that Hale, Edward's aide-de-camp and military secretary, "has been upwards of seven years in my family, and from the number of years he has served, and the very little promotion he has obtained in the course of his Service, he has strong claims for some provision."[298]

Because Edward Augustus made extensive efforts to dispense patronage, it would likely be unwise to read too much into the Prince's letters of recommendation. However, it is also unlikely that the Prince was unaware of Wentworth's suspicions or completely ignorant of the situation within the Maroon establishment. While this does not in any way suggest that Prince Edward was implicated in the anti-settlement faction, his recommendations, even if they were not acted upon, must have been galling to Sir John Wentworth. At the same time, however, the Prince also maintained close and friendly relations with Wentworth, from whom he leased his residence on Bedford Basin.

In the midst of these charges, countercharges, and spirited defences, the business of the Maroons went on, though the management of their "Establishment" remained unsettled. Alexander Howe was unpopular with the Maroons[299] and "soon after this appointment they again relapsed into idleness, and labour was neglected for amusements, for cards and cockfighting, strolling to town, and occasionally earning some money in accidental occupations."[300]

In December 1797 Wentworth appointed Chamberlain, the schoolmaster, "to guide and carry into effect the agriculture duties of the Maroons,"[301] and waited through another long and severe winter with "more that 6 1/2 feet of snow on a level thro' the country." This broadening of Chamberlain's responsibility was perhaps due to Wentworth's increasing concern over the inactivity of the Maroons under Howe's direction and to the demands of both Jamaica and Britain that the Maroons be more self-sufficient. Perhaps, too, the acquisition of more land, the Cochran Estate, demanded that more attention be given to agriculture than Howe had to give.

In March Wentworth noted that the Maroons are "quiet and orderly, alto' some are still wicked eno' [sic] to endeavor to make them discontented."[302] In April he promised to "avoid committing Government to any responsibility for their expense."[303]

Howe and his family spent the year in residence at Maroon Hall in relative comfort, entertaining guests,[304] managing as he could and, like the Maroons, waiting out the winter. For many of the Maroons, however, the experience of a second harsh winter in Nova Scotia reinforced their determination to leave. T.C. Haliburton states:

> Whatever solicitations of being settled for life in the Province, might have been made by them in the summer of

1797, their desire of removal was revived during the winter,
...[and that they] continued refractory, and the Governor
... began with some reason to be weary of his charge, and
heartily to repent the encouragement he had given to their
remaining in Nova Scotia.[305]

Apparently aware of the situation, Wentworth decided that Captain
Howe was more needed elsewhere. In a letter of 9 July 1798 Wentworth
informed him, "The object of your appointment in the offices of the
Maroons, being so far accomplished, and the indispensable justice and
necessity of reducing every possible expense in that establishment, con-
curring to make it my duty to suppress your Agency and department at
Maroon Hall altogether and entirely."[306] On the same day he asked the
more forceful Theophilus Chamberlain to take charge of the affairs of
the Maroons, adding, "Altho I have thus added to your business, I cannot add to your salary" and directed him to "forthwith cause the
Maroons to do their statute labours on the roads, work on their farms,
and cause them to go to Church and the children to school."[307]

Chamberlain's appointment might have brought some stability to
the office, but he "found them as exasperating as they found life in
Preston."[308] At least he was spared the further complication of the pres-
ence of Captain John Hale who returned to England in 1798, as did
Prince Edward Augustus. Unlike the Prince, Hale did not return to
Nova Scotia.[309]

In November Wentworth, while still protesting to the British government the July 1798 decision of Jamaica to withhold further financial assistance, claimed "that the Maroons are nearly reclaimed from
the erroneous impressions, and wild, impracticable expectations introduced among them by artful insidious persons," and pointed out, "The
expensive establishment bro't here, and entered into by the Agents who
accompanied and conducted their affairs for account and in behalf, of
the Island of Jamaica, are either suppressed or reduced."[310] By late 1798,
however, the future of the Maroons was no longer in the hands of Sir
John Wentworth. Whether encouraged or discouraged, he had largely

"run out his line." The weather and a ructious, divisive administration had made success difficult. While it might be erroneous to assume that a united front and a commonality of purpose among the colonial officials responsible for the Maroons would have meant their successful settlement in Nova Scotia, there can be little doubt that this division of purpose contributed greatly to its failure. These, however, were not the only problems.

CHAPTER 8

Internal Disputes and the Creation of Boydville

Disputes within the Maroon community were as marked as were the divisions among the superintendents of the Maroon establishment. While the cohesiveness of the Maroons was demonstrated by their determination to share each other's fate when the majority faced exile from Jamaica, and while this decision was largely duplicated when the Maroons left Nova Scotia, it should not be supposed that internal harmony prevailed. Undoubtedly, the external pressures of contested leadership added to the internal problems of the Maroon community; but it seems clear that many of the same problems would have existed anyway. In a warrior society, where fighting each other seemed to be only slightly less attractive than fighting together, arguments could easily lead to disagreements and disagreements to vendetta.

Sir John Wentworth was not ignorant of the situation within the community. In 1797 he complained to the Duke of Clarence that the Maroons "do not wish to live by industry — but prefer war and hunting which would render them very dangerous in any other country but this." He further contended:

> [B]eing well fed during the winter, they create little troubles to themselves, being naturally capricious and cunning[.] Among themselves they are divided into three parties or tribes, not loving each other, and extremely jealous lest preference should be given to any — From these sources are derived all the troubles they really know. [311]

While Wentworth's conclusion might be questioned, there is no doubt but that some of these "little troubles" had ongoing consequences. One Maroon, surnamed Williams, "in the issue of a week's perpetual quarrel with his wife, did in a fit of passion, suddenly cut his throat,"[312] while others complained of being "waked and kept awake almost every night with drunken family squabbles."[313]

Some disputes lingered even after the Maroons had left Nova Scotia. While in Maroon Town (Preston), Elsy Jarrett, the daughter or niece of Maroon Captain Jarrett, described variously by Wentworth as a "sensible old man"[314] and as one of the leaders of "their folly,"[315] laid a complaint against a Maroon named William Barnet who, she claimed, had assaulted her. Theophilus Chamberlain and two Maroon captains heard the charge and two other Maroon captains had "become Bail for the appearance of the said Barnet in case any injury befell the said Elsy within a certain limited span."

On board the *Asia*, en route to Sierra Leone, on 10 September 1800, George Ross noted in his journal, "Elsy Jarrett is delivered of a son today — the father of it is Charles Shaw. It seems this young adventurer has come forth before his time, and Jarrett vows if the child should die before he is an old man, Barnet must be brought to justice for it."

Jarrett's threat against the man who had given his kin "the thumping," which he apparently felt had caused the premature birth of her child, was not one to be taken lightly. Barnet's apparent predilection for violence later led to his murder of two Maroon women shortly after their arrival in Sierra Leone and, in reaction, his suicide.[316] In his journal Ross, who served as Superintendent of the Maroons during their voyage from Nova Scotia to Africa and for a short time in Sierra Leone, made various references to the violence of the Maroons in their relationship with each other — a violence that undoubtedly had occurred in Nova Scotia as well.[317]

At least part of the cause of the quarrels and the violence could be attributed to the vast quantity of rum consumed by the Maroons. The over-consumption of alcohol was certainly not unique to the Maroons during the last years of the eighteenth century in Halifax:

The West Indies trade had flooded the town with cheap

rum, much of it made from molasses imported by two Halifax distilleries. These turned out ninety thousand gallons a year ... [and] Rum was to be had in every store as well as in the numerous taverns and dives. The household keg in the cellar with its spigot and mug were as common a sight as the potato bin or the barrel of salt herring.[318]

So great was the scourge of rum that the Halifax clergyman Reverend Dr. Mather Byles, who was described as paternalistic, somewhat puritanical, cynical, and cantankerous,[319] had pronounced that "rheumatisms and rum-atisms are the two most endemical diseases of Halifax."[320]

"Rum-atism" was a disease that affected all levels of society. For example, Prince William, brother to Prince Edward Augustus who was always sober, during one of his sojourns in the port city, according to the recollection of one of his junior officers, had, one night, "proposed twenty eight toasts, drank each one in a bumper of champagne and claret, then added fourteen bottles of ale as a chaser, after which he 'sang two or three songs and for three hours laughed incessantly'."[321]

However, in both Nova Scotia and Sierra Leone, it seems that every Maroon occasion, whether birth, death or intervening event, was marked by drinking and often by drunkenness. At Preston there were complaints about the Maroons' enjoyment of "Indolence, Cockfighting and Gaming"[322] and of rum, especially on Sundays and holy days. [323] George Ross noted:

> Lawrence's wife died today. George, her son, being well in my opinion, and pledging himself for any noise that would ensue, I gave him in advance 3 Gallons of Rum — more particularly, as we cannot have a coffin in time to have her out of the way tonight — and the Maroons have no ideas of letting their dead enjoy the *sweets of solitude*, until they are under-ground.[324]

While many people considered that rum was almost a necessity of life in the hostile climate of Nova Scotia and prodigious quantities were consumed by all, the Maroons, to whom it was native drink, seem to have surpassed even the common appetite for it.[325] Indeed, among the Maroons' first complaints about life in Nova Scotia was not only that "the fine fruits of Jamaica were no longer within their reach, and the variety of vegetables, which nature had hitherto so abundantly produced for them, were now exchanged for potatoes alone," but that "Sugar and Rum, were given out with a sparing hand." While they were provided with necessities, the "luxuries, many of which were by habit become almost necessaries, they were now to bid a long adieu."[326]

Another cause of dispute within the Maroon community was over the apportioning of blame for their exile to Nova Scotia. While the governor and government of Jamaica were considered the chief villains,[327] some of the Maroons themselves were also blamed. In a letter to General George Walpole, Maroon captain Andrew Smith acknowledged, "That he is very much blamed by the rest of the Maroons for deceiving them with promises, and [accused] of having received money from you to betray them. That such is his situation on that account, that he verily believes they would kill him."[328] Elsewhere, Captain Smith, in correspondence with his brother, Charles Samuels, who was then in England,[329] complained about the difficulty of maintaining "such a large family as ours ... You know I have 4 wives and 8 small children besides our father, old Toe Williams and our mother, sisters we have plenty and there is only you and Cope and myself to maintain 18 or 20." Compounding his problems, Smith confided to his brother, was "how strong parties run against me and the rest of our family for being the cause of bringing in the Maroons and surrendering their arms in the Treaty" that ended the last Maroon War in Jamaica.[330] Moreover, in Maroon Town he had agreed "to do what good I can in reconciling the Maroons to the country." "Smith was to carry the suspicion of 'traitor' with him to Nova Scotia and Sierra Leone."[331]

Under such pressure it is not surprising that the community began to crack. Indeed, some who had joined their fellows in exile, although they were exempt from the punishment, had by 1797 begun to question the wisdom of their decision and began to explore the possibility of returning to Jamaica.[332] The crack became a split, however, as a result of Alexander Ochterlony's apparent efforts to prove the Nova Scotia Maroon experiment a failure. After convincing the Maroons that if they did not work (and indeed obtaining an oath from them that they would not work so long as they were in Preston) they would be taken elsewhere, Ochterlony moved to convince any "backsliders" of their folly.[333]

In 1798 Alexander Howe reported, "One James William Dunbar a Maroon has told me he was punished and confined to the Bilboas [sic] by Mr. Ochterlony for cutting wood or fencing poles in the winter for some inhabitant." Others were threatened with the loss of provisions and some were forced to divide their wages with those who had refused to work.[334] One group, "a family more industrious than the Most (Palmers at Cole Harbour)", planted potatoes, "and for so doing incurred Mr. O[chterlony]'s displeasure, and the Maroons at Preston were so exasperated at them it was thought by Mr. Q[uarrell] [that it was] no longer safe for them to Continue at Cole Harbour and [he] removed them."[335] Alexander Howe stated in 1797 that "none are inclined to separate from their families or be at any distance from the main Body of these People,"[336] but the separation of the community nonetheless took place.

Either because of their decision to work on their farms, or their nominal acceptance of Christianity, or because of their family connections, a group requested to be separated from "their unregenerated brothers."[337] On 10 July 1797 Wentworth informed his superiors that "one family of twenty-eight persons led by a noted Captain, removes this day to a separate Estate, at his own earnest request,[338] where they immediately showed great alacrity in working for themselves."[339] The "noted Captain" was James Palmer. He was one of the last hold-out leaders in the Jamaican war and had "breathed war and defiance." He and another leader, Leonard Parkinson, were described as "intrepid." They were "two of the outstanding leaders of the war, with their activities repeatedly mentioned in the official documents."[340] Palmer commanded a reward of £100 for his capture, dead or alive. Parkinson's was £50. Writing to Balcarres, Walpole warned, "If Palmer or Parkinson should refuse the terms, which I think they will, you will never conquer them."[341]

Palmer, the war hero, had now opted for peace, and the "separate Estate" was called Boydville. The 1000-acre Boydville Farm had been purchased by Quarrell and Ochterlony in February 1797. The land had been a portion of the grant made to James Douglas and Patrick West in 1763, and transferred to John Cunningham that same year. Cunningham sold "Lotts [sic] Number Twelve and Thirteen lying and being on the Road leading from Fort Sackville to Windsor" to George F. Boyd of Halifax in December 1784. It was his widow, Elizabeth, who sold Boydville Farm thirteen years later. This land, or part of it, as the Crown Land Index shows, is today known as Maroon Hill.[342]

The "small band of hard-working, Christian converts" at Boydville was a "model of Wentworth's hopes."[343] In 1798 he wrote, "They are progressing in cultivating their lands, with zeal and industry"[344] and are "pursuing their husbandry, with great cheerfulness and ingenuity, and will soon be comfortably independent in their circumstances."[345] Later, when complaining about the Maroons in general, Wentworth exempted those at Boydville, writing, "The Maroons still refuse to work on their plantations, except those at Boydville."[346] All of them would "however, labour on the roads, and for Farmers, Merchants, etc. [347] ... and the Women and Children supply the Market [at Halifax] with Berries — eggs — poultry — etc., by which they gain great profit, in aid of their support."[348] These items, together with the sale of "pigs, Brooms and Baskets," supplemented the government support that the Boydville group, which had grown to at least sixty by 1799, needed least of all. While the Preston Maroons petitioned for removal, those at Boydville requested "Some Sheep ... as we observe them to be very productive in the Hands of the people about us; — and, some seed Grain; and a cow or two." In addition, they wanted an opportunity for their children to receive instruction, "being so far from the School at Preston, that none of them have been able to profit by it."[349]

However, despite disputes, differences and disagreements, the sense of community was very strong, and while internal disputes might have caused a split, external pressures drew them back together. When all the Maroons were to be removed from Nova Scotia, Wentworth privately hoped that "Palmer's Boydville blacks might nonetheless refuse to go."[350] But go they would. "Altho," Wentworth explained, "their Habits of acquaintance and their family connection and relationships with the others who reside at Preston overcomes their judgement and wishes," the community again came together. This is not to suggest the rift was healed. The Boydville group was still wary and "they earnestly entreated to be embarked in a vessel separate and to be located in a country at least fifteen miles distant from the others, whose conduct they have so much disapproved, that they say, they must fight if together."[351]

CHAPTER 9

Financial Complications and Political Problems

To compound Wentworth's problems with the settlement of the Maroons was the official concern over his management of their financial affairs. Financial problems, however, were an almost perpetual part of Wentworth's life. Brian Cuthbertson, Wentworth's biographer, points out that from his college days at Harvard to the day of his death, Wentworth lived a bare step from insolvency and more than once he was forced to flee to escape debtor's prison. Nonetheless, "he lived extremely well" and "borrowed heavily in anticipation"[352] of inheritance, of redress of losses, of recovering debts, or of receiving back wages. All the while he and Lady Wentworth "entertained and were entertained and they spent far beyond their means."[353]

> But money was plentiful because of war expenditures, and the times were gay. There was a round of genteel entertainment led by Sir John and Lady Wentworth at Government House and patronized by Prince Edward and Madame [de St-Laurent]. Edward also dined with the national societies, danced at the balls, and attended the plays ... The well to do ... held their teas, card parties, and routs ... One chronicler wrote: 'Balls were almost a daily occurrence with such a show of beauty as hardly any other town could exhibit. The dazzling white shoulders of the Archdeacon's daughters, the bright eyes and elegant figures of the four Miss Cunards, the fair complexions and sweet expressions of the four Miss Uniackes all whirled before one, happy with the arm of a red or blue-coated gallant encircling their waists'.[354]

Despite the gaity, by the early 1790s the Wentworths faced financial ruin in consequence of their own impecuniousness and as a result of placing too much trust in cousin Paul Wentworth's handling of their financial affairs. Wentworth's appointment to the governorship of Nova Scotia in 1792 should have brought some financial security, but "as usual with the Wentworths they spent up to their expectations."[355]

Wentworth's personal financial situation and his penchant for direct action without and, sometimes, against authority provides the background for the financial situation attending the "Maroon debacle." This is not to suggest that Wentworth was dishonest. Brian Cuthbertson writes:

> During the eighteen years of his governorship some £160,000 of expenditures, mostly war-related, in addition to the normal governmental spending, had passed through Wentworth's hands. All of this had to be minutely accounted for under the new treasury regulations. But he had been able to afford only a small staff to assist him, at times probably only one clerk. Much of the accounting he had to do himself. He hated the drudgery involved and found it demeaning to his dignity as a royal governor of such long service. He expected his superiors to trust his judgement that the expenditures were necessary and that he was honest, and as far as can be determined he was honest. The accounting demands made on Wentworth would have overwhelmed all but the most expert accountant, and Wentworth was certainly not that.[356]

Wentworth might not have been a good accountant, but he was no less accountable for the expenditures he made, sometimes without permission, on behalf of the Maroons — expenditures that ultimately resulted in the suspension of his salary and left his "personal finances in shambles."[357]

Early in the Maroon experiment, when the Jamaican government was financially liable for the bills of the Maroons, Wentworth's unauthorized and sometimes rash expenditures could be overlooked by his London masters. However, when Jamaica threatened to withdraw or to limit further assistance, the Duke of Portland, under attack in the House of Commons, turned on Wentworth in 1798 and "refused to approve the new bills Wentworth had drawn for the Maroons."[358] Wentworth, apparently assured of the rightness of his position, and despite Portland's warning that "no Part of the Charge on their account, can possibly be borne by this Country,"[359] charged other costs incurred by the Maroon settlement to the British Government, and, when they were repudiated, he was held personally responsible for their payment.[360] The anonymous letters which charged Wentworth with personally profiting from the purchase of flour for use by the Maroons and, with the creation of an extensive and expensive "Maroon Establishment," squandering the monies meant to support the settlement of the Maroons, further troubled Wentworth's relationship with Britain. While the accusation about the flour was demonstrated to be without foundation and the other claims exaggerated, they pointed to the growing costs and other problems related to the settlement of the Trelawnys.[361]

These concerns were not confined to the Secretary of State for the Colonies and his British and overseas officials. While the concerns of the local Assembly had been placated by Wentworth's self-confidence and Jamaican largesse, Members' questions about the Maroons were to re-echo over the next twenty-four months in both Nova Scotia and Britain; and perhaps the most serious challenge to Wentworth's plans for the Maroons was the ongoing attention their affairs received in the British Parliament. General Walpole, the victor of the Maroon War, had returned to Great Britain deeply insulted by the affront to his honour when his personal promise to the Maroons was ignored by the Jamaican government and he was determined to bring political attention to the issue.

As early as October 1796 Charles James Fox, leader of the Whig Opposition in the House of Commons and a personal friend of

General Walpole, asked the House "whether the Jamacian government had not broken faith with the Maroons and from that point forward, he, Walpole, and William Wilberforce … kept the Maroon issue alive in Parliament."[362] When Walpole was elected to Parliament he became a vocal member of the opposition and sought topics, especially the Maroons, to embarrass the Pitt administration. Walpole was also a friend of George Tierney, who served as the leader of the opposition when Fox was absent from the House, and in May 1798 Walpole acted as his second when Tierney challenged Prime Minister William Pitt to a duel. In turn, Tierney seconded anything and everything when Walpole spoke about the Maroons.

Walpole began his efforts to force a debate on the Maroons in February 1798, but because of the stalling tactics of the government benches, "he did not succeed with a full-dressed debate" until May 1798. "And indeed this was the only real debate which gave Walpole the opportunity to make his views known before the Maroons were finally sent to Sierra Leone."[363] His efforts, to debate their deportation from Jamaica, their settlement in Nova Scotia, or to introduce their numerous petitions to Parliament, cannot be considered a success. While Walpole "invariably spoke with too much warmth and revealed more than once that his concern was more for his honour than for the Maroons," the issue needled the government and was dangerous to Wentworth's position in Nova Scotia. Walpole, "determined to get all the Maroons' complaints into the record," read the James petition of August 1797 to the House and moved to have the earlier June petition laid before it. After parliamentary wrangling about whether such a petition ever existed and if it did, was it a petition to the House or simply a request to him, Walpole moved that the House "debate whether or not the negotiations he had held with the Maroons had been honoured properly."[364] He charged the Jamacian government with an act of "gross inhumanity" by sending the Maroons from the heat of the tropics to the cold of Nova Scotia.

The government was prepared for the challenge and in a series of arguments refuted Walpole's motion for a special debate. First, they contended, the movement of the Maroons was an internal affair of the Jamaican government and within their area of responsibility; second, they pointed out that Wentworth was an experienced and trusted royal governor and well able to manage the settlement of the Maroons; and third, they insisted the government of Jamaica had been very liberal in their support of the Maroon exiles and had expended nearly £50,000 on their aid. The government then went on the attack and revealed that Walpole had wished to settle the Trelawny Maroons in the lowlands near Spanish Town "where the access to spirits will soon decrease their numbers, and destroy that hearty constitution which is nourished by a healthy mountainous situation."[365] Was this, they asked, more honourable than Wentworth's care and protection of the Maroons in Nova Scotia? The embarrassed Walpole could only respond with requests for confirmation of the Jamaican expenditure on the Maroons and his motion failed by over a 6 to 1 ratio.[366]

Having won that round, the Duke of Portland and the government were determined that their fate was not going to rest on the pleasure of the Maroons, and, according to Winks' colourful metaphor, Wentworth and Portland came to realize "that neither of them could be Ezekiel nor the Maroons their valley of dry bones."[367] Despite assurances from Wentworth about the future prospects of the Maroons, Portland decided to act. Wentworth continued to hope for the best, but

> the dissatisfaction early created among them was still fostered by their pretended friends, or by those who wished their absence. They were acquainted with the proceedings of the Assembly of Jamaica and the subsequent occurrences; they thought themselves injured, and passed the winter of 1799 in discontent and murmurs.[368]

The petitions presented to the British government were likely conveyed to England by a Maroon named Charles Samuels who had participated in the Trelawny Town rebellion and had apparently been one of the few rebels who had "come in" during the limited time allowed by the treaty that ended the Maroon War of 1795-96. He then likely joined his brother Captain Andrew Smith in the effort to convince his fellow Maroons to surrender to General George Walpole.[369] He, together with an otherwise unidentified Maroon woman, referred to only as Sue (and once as Eve),[370] was employed in the service of the victorious General Walpole. Both Samuels and Sue were among the exiled Maroons who landed in Halifax in July 1796 and settled in Preston. Walpole, however, did not forget them. On 22 September 1796 he wrote to William Quarrell explaining that he had obtained permission from the British home secretary, the Duke of Portland, "to send for any of the Maroons I please." Walpole further explained that he had "agreed to take ... Charles Samuels into my service," and asked Quarrell, "if he chooses to come here to me, to have him taken care of on board some merchant ship coming to London, and draw on Messrs. Walpole and Co., Lombard Street, London, for the expense, to be charged to my account."[371]

The delays that necessarily attended transportation and communication in the 1790s meant that the fall of 1796 became the spring of 1797 before Samuels, and perhaps Sue, could leave Nova Scotia. By then, the Maroons, discontented with the prospects of life in Maroon Town, and alarmed with the severity of the weather, were in communication with General Walpole, "representing their situation as untenable in Nova Scotia."[372] In April 1797 Quarrell reminded the Jamaican Agent in London that "General Walpole has had the Duke of Portland's permission to send for two Maroons," and informed him that "one goes home in the packet with Colonel Leonard."[373]

Charles Samuels was caught up in the "intrigue" against settlement in Nova Scotia and was commissioned by his brother, Andrew Smith, and Maroon Colonel Montague James, to carry to England the 23 April 1797 "Maroon Petition to General Walpole," and perhaps as well, "The humble Petition of the Unfortunate Maroons" on "behalf of 530 Maroons," both of which pleaded for their removal from Nova Scotia. In addition, Samuels carried private verbal and written requests to Walpole, reminding him that his word on their expulsion had been broken, as well as of their attendant problems.

Wentworth later charged that "the Samuels' expedition was unauthorized" and that his departure bearing secret petitions was part of the intrigue against their settlement which had been hatched by Alexander Ochterlony, supported by military officers Leonard and others, and countenanced by Quarrell himself.[374] The Samuels expedition, however, was authorized, as was attested to in a letter from Portland to General Walpole on 19 October 1797 in which he admitted that "the Maroons in question came here by permission," and by Quarrell's statement that he had informed Sir John Wentworth "many weeks before he sailed" that Samuels "was to go to England with Colonel Leonard."[375]

The date of the messenger's arrival in London is not recorded. However, on 3 June 1797, Captain Andrew Smith addressed a letter from Nova Scotia to his brother, then in England, trusting that Charles had already seen General Walpole and informing him that "in a few weeks hence I shall look very anxiously for a letter from you."[376] It seems that by then Samuels and Sue had already carried out their responsibilities as messengers, for by July 1797 Walpole had sent "some papers. . .relative to the Maroons to the Duke of Portland."[377] Deeply insulted by the affront to his honour when his personal promise to the Maroons was ignored by the Island government, Walpole had used his influence in Parliament to draw attention to the issue. As early as October 1796 the radical Whig opposition had introduced the subject of the Maroons in the House of Commons. Upon his election, Walpole himself used every opportunity to speak about the Maroons, although it was not always clear whether it was to protect them or to defend his own insulted honour. Moreover, Walpole was annoyed that the Home Secretary would not compensate him for paying the passage of Samuels and Sue to England. He had "been asking for indemnification ... for the sake of common bare justice," but without success, even after several letters.

The government stalled, questioned, and delayed on every point raised in the Maroon petition. In March 1798 Portland enquired of Walpole whether the "paper purporting to be the Petition of the

Maroons to His Majesty," which had reportedly been "delivered by the hands of the Maroons whom I had permitted to come to you from Halifax, he being commissioned by his Brethren to do so," could be ascertained by the Maroon in question as being authentic.[378] However, as Portland likely already knew, on 6 April 1798, "In a laconic note, Walpole sardonically reminded the Duke that it was not possible for him to put the question to the messenger Maroon since he had already returned to Halifax."[379]

Just when Charles Samuels (and Sue, although her name disappears from the records) returned to Halifax is unclear. In 1799 Wentworth, explaining that the Samuels expedition was contrary to his wishes and complaining that it was "leading to mischief only, and impossible to produce any good," provided the next chapter in the story of Charles Samuels:

> On his passage from England, he was captured by the French, and for several months resided in France, where he was treated with great kindness and attention; which had exceedingly engaged his attachment and affection; as he himself told Sir. J. Wentworth.[380]

Sir John went on to report that the French had made "very many inquiries … about Maroons and Jamaica," information which Samuels had "artfully declined" to communicate to the Governor "though he did not deny." Wentworth concluded, "Time can only develop what information he gave — certain it is however, that neither the British government, nor the island of Jamaica, are much obliged to Mr. Quarrell and his colleague for being the cause of so dangerous an event."

CHAPTER 10

The Sierra Leone Option

Wentworth's hopes for establishing the Maroons finally ran out in the spring of 1799. Unknown to him, the Duke of Portland had opened negotiations with the Sierra Leone Company to determine whether the colony of Sierra Leone in western Africa, the 1792 destination of the Nova Scotian black loyalists, could be the new home of the Maroons. Portland, who had survived the political difficulties in the British House of Commons over the Maroons, wished to ensure that they would not again become the subject of debate. The Maroons had "become a dead weight upon the hands of His Majesty's Government, …their subsistence amounting to no less a sum that [*sic*] ten thousand pounds a year."[381] Accordingly, by January of 1799, Portland was in correspondence with the officers of the Company about Sierra Leone, which had earlier been considered as a possible destination for the Maroons. Winks observes:

> Early in January 1799, Henry Thornton sent a new petition from the Maroons to Portland, and he may have received it from Walpole via Wilberforce. Certainly the initiative came from Nova Scotia; equally certainly it did not come from Wentworth, who was genuinely surprised when he learned in May that negotiations for the transfer of the Maroons already were well advanced.[382]

By March 1799, while still concerned about attendant expenses, Portland's negotiations with the Company had advanced to the point that he asserted, "I cannot hesitate in expressing my wishes, that no time should be lost in taking the necessary steps for accomplishing so desirable an object."[383] On 22 March 1799 the Sierra Leone Company agreed to the terms of settlement of the Maroons in their Colony with the following suggestion:

> That the Maroons and Nova Scotians should be placed at a sufficient distance to prevent that jealousy between the two bodies that We fear will be too easily excited in each and also to remove the danger of our being assailed at any time by the joint complaints of these two descriptions of People and of our being attacked by the turbulent and disaffected of each party with their united force.[384]

Advanced as these plans were, Wentworth was still in the dark. Indeed, in April he had complained, "Those at Preston are still deluded with false schemes of returning to Jamaica, where they may gratify their revenge" and fumed, "Wicked as their ideas are, they find some wicked enough to encourage them — and to advise them not work or plant, or do anything toward their own support." In the late spring of 1799 Wentworth again apportioned the blame for the difficulty of settling the Maroons:

> Mr. Ochterlony, conceived the horrid scheme of removing them by and with Arms, to make an establishment in some African climate and prevailed on Capt. Hale to countenance and support the Measure, which has been artfully pursued, to this Hour, with a Diligence and Address, which have caused all the Trouble, and increased the Expense. [385]

While the Boydville settlers continued to labour, those at Preston did not and Wentworth reported in April that he had "ordered Provisions to be stopped, until they were returned to work and as one of them threatened to kill some of the Cattle — I tho't it best to order Captain Solomon with one Subaltern and thirty men, to do duty two or three days at Preston."[386] Wentworth went on to report:

The party proceeded, and the next day Captain Solomon returned to Town with part of the Detatchment, leaving Lieutenant Muller with twelve men, As there hath not been the least attempt to resist or commit violence, I did not request Brigadier General Murray to augment the Post — he has however tho't it necessary to increase Captain Solomon's party of the Royal Nova Scotia Regiment to fifty men . . . . I am confident no violence is intended — nor does any such apprehensions exist among the white inhabitants in the village.[387]

While order could be maintained, the troops could not stop gossip or limit the spread of rumours.

On 30 May 1799 Wentworth again complained to Portland that just when he had convinced the Preston Maroons to return to cultivation, and to "wiser considerations" his hopes were dashed by rumours about the Sierra Leone negotiations. He wrote:

[T]heir last hope it now appears, was placed on the Exertions of Captain Hale, to cause their Petition, secretly composed, signed and committed to him, to be presented to Parliament, who, they were assured, beyond all doubt, would meet the Wishes of the poor, suffering Maroons — No news of the event arriving as soon as was expected — the good effect on their conduct and conversation was evident. Unfortunately before the Spring, (this year three weeks later than usual) was advanced eno' for their husbandry — The Packet arrived, and they received intelligence that Captain Hale had prevailed over the Governor — and presented their Petition which, they are assured of has been patronized — the Signers instantly communicated their news to the rest, and all agreed not to work this year — soon after this resolution, a Vessel arrived from Jamaica, from whence they derived additional causes of perverseness

— and about the same time another Packet arrived bringing news of a negotiation with the Sierra Leone Company to remove them, to their Possessions in Africa — That this will certainly take place — they most certainly believe, and will not be persuaded — That I have not received Your Graces command to that purpose.[388]

Stripped of any credibility, Wentworth could not convince the Preston Maroons otherwise and they, unlike those at Boydville, refused to "work on their plantations." Again Wentworth reported that he had "caused the Rations to be withheld for several weeks — while refractory, and shall again resort to that measure, as it may be usefully applied, until it is determined whither they are to be removed to Sierra Leone, which is reported, and they rely upon so much."[389]

By then the die was cast: "By secret letter on June 10, Portland at last told Sir John Wentworth of his plans: Walpole and the Preston Maroons had won." Complaining of the heavy expense and with no certainty of the Maroons ever being assimilated into Nova Scotia, Portland informed Wentworth that His Majesty's Government had negotiated an agreement with the Sierra Leone Company to resettle the Maroons. The Crown would pay for their transportation, settlement and education, and the Company would provide lands and administer the move.

Wentworth was ordered to keep the plan a secret from the Maroons (obviously a vain hope) and advised that the ship *Asia* would arrive in October to remove them. He was instructed "to sell their land and houses as advantageously as possible after they left." Wentworth was further commanded that "the wishes of the Maroons were not to be considered; not one Maroon was to be permitted to remain in Nova Scotia." Even those at Boydville, who Wentworth continued to laud for their efforts, were to leave and if they were fearful of "travel on the same vessel as the Preston Maroons, measures could be taken to see to it that no one carried a weapon aboard ship."[390]

Wentworth's hopes were dashed, his health affected,[391] and his great effort was a failure. His character had been assaulted, his honesty questioned, his judgement queried, and his competence assailed over his handling of the Maroon settlement. He must have felt that his enemies had not only succeeded but that they had undermined his position within the colonial service of the British government. Publicly he held his peace but privately he felt wronged.

His wife, Frances Wentworth, in correspondence with Lady Fitzwilliam, her close friend in England, complained that the Duke of Portland "has conducted himself with great duplicity," a view Lady Wentworth no doubt shared with her husband.[392] Winks concludes that a variety of forces combined to defeat Wentworth. Obviously, the James-Walpole-Jamaican connection was at the heart of it. In addition:

> Many whites in Nova Scotia hoped to see Wentworth brought low, for as Surveyor-General of the King's Woods he had prevented speculation in land, and as a genuinely humane governor he had extended aid to penurious Indians as well as to the Maroons. Those who were not included in the gay social life he and his Lady, Frances, brought to the capital, or who were excluded from his patronage, encouraged the Maroons to complain of 'unfelt distress,' for they were one more means by which Wentworth might be attacked.[393]

Perhaps in frustration, or perhaps in response to the earlier charges that he had to defend himself against, in June 1799 Wentworth went on the attack. He wrote to the Governor of Jamaica and laid a number of charges against William Dawes Quarrell, the former commissary of the Maroons. In "A Statement of Facts respecting the settling of the Maroons in Nova Scotia," Wentworth's charges ranged from misrepresentation to misconduct, from the taint of dishonesty to the charge of complicity, and Quarrell was asked by the Jamaican Assembly to respond to eighteen of them. In his response Quarrell was every bit as eloquent and spirited in his own defence as Wentworth had been the year before. In these sometimes petty and generally unsavoury charges and countercharges, truth was likely an early victim, but they do provide an interesting perspective of what each perceived, or at least represented, as his role in the period that they had worked together.[394]

During the summer and early fall of 1799 Wentworth undertook the fulfilment of his orders. While he continued to inform Portland that the Preston Maroons "are disinclined to work on their own farms," he was able to add, "They however labour on the roads, and for Farmers, Merchants, etc." The eternal optimist, he could not refrain from adding that this work would "gradually turn them to perceive more advantages in cultivating for themselves, if the contemplated plans reported, for their removal to Africa, should not take place and their settlement here to be finally commanded."[395] However, despite these and similar comments, Wentworth ensured that all of the Maroons were accounted for and that they would be prepared to leave when transportation was available. In December 1799 he again assured Portland that "care shall be taken that they are all embarked for Africa, according to their own repeated and continued requests, and your Grace's instructions."[396]

While most of the Maroons lived within a few miles of Halifax, some had moved elsewhere. Early in their settlement in Nova Scotia, William Cottnam Tonge had asked permission to settle some of them on his lands. Either because this conflicted with his belief that the Maroons should be kept together or because he intensely disliked Tonge, who he believed had "not a little assisted in their discontent,"[397] Wentworth rejected his request. Later, when he was able to report that all of the Maroons were ready to leave at an hour's notice, he noted the exception of "two families, who say they have engaged with Mr. Tonge, and will stay with him." On this point Wentworth was pleased to adhere to his orders if only because he believed that "while government contemplated their settlement here, Mr. Tonge took part with those who instructed them to resist."[398] Likewise, when "Captain Andrew Smith and Family alledge [sic] that the Island of Jamaica engaged to readmit them," Wentworth, because he had no confirmation of this claim, refused to allow them to leave, "especially, as they are a resolute, acute Family, and possess great knowledge of the Island, and influence among the Negroes."[399] In any event, Wentworth was determined that "neither Mr. Tonge nor the Maroons shall be suffered to frustrate my instructions to send them *all* to Africa."[400]

The greatest frustration for Wentworth was, however, the failure of the HMS *Asia*, which was to transport the Maroons, to arrive. The ship, scheduled to arrive in Halifax in October, was late. On 22 October 1799 Wentworth reported that the *Asia* "was spoke to about 14 days since, going up the River St. Lawrence, where it is probable she will arrive in time to embark one of the Regiments ordered to Halifax ... to proceed under convoy of His Majesty's armed Brig *Earl of Moira* sent from hence for that purpose."[401] Wentworth's hope that the transport would arrive in Halifax "in ten to sixteen days" was disappointed. In December he informed Portland:

> The ship Asia had a long Passage and struck on the Transverses in going up to Quebec, and being detained to convey the 26 Regiment to this place, the Seamen dissatisfied, and apprehensions were entertained of the lateness of the season to navigate through the Gulf on these coasts, so many deserted and were disabled by sickness, that the Pilots refused to take charge of the ship, and it is reported, for no official letters are yet received, that the troops are disembarked and the ship haled [sic] up, and secured for the Winter. It is much to be feared that the Ship will suffer much damage from the ice, to which she must be much exposed.[402]

Wentworth, acting against his orders to do nothing, immediately sought private transports that could be chartered to take the Maroons to Africa. Fortunately for Wentworth, none was available at the price he was prepared to authorize and consequently the Maroons were destined to spend another winter in Nova Scotia. "Portland's insistence on speed had merely led to more antagonism between whites and blacks in

Nova Scotia, since all had expected to be rid of the problem long before Christmas."[403]

Despite the disappointment, however, the winter passed without undue duress. Chamberlain again had his responsibilities increased when Jonathon (a.k.a. John) Moody left the "Establishment." However, as "Clarke [sic] and Issuer of Provisions, Clothing and Stores" from 30 September 1799 to 30 September 1800, Chamberlain did receive an additional £50 salary per annum as compensation.[404]

Because Dr. Oxley had departed for England, Wentworth arranged for Dr. John Fraser to provide medical attention to the Maroons. Wentworth was able to report that "they are in good health, and give me no further trouble, than the care of subsisting them, and some casual attentions to circumstances, which must naturally generate among six hundred people, in society."[405] In addition to the administrations of Dr. Fraser, Wentworth authorized the payment of £33.13.11 to Dr. Michael Head "for medicine and services to sick and infirm Maroons."[406]

Again, contrary to orders, he purchased "thirty eight pipes [104.95 gallons] of high proof Brandy and forty hogsheads of Tobacco" for the Maroons.[407] These luxuries were repudiated by an angry Lord Portland who ordered Wentworth to sell them, which Wentworth promised to do, with the cheerful comment, "I expect without loss to Government."[408] As Robin Winks wrote, "Authority, however, was not easily placated and eventually Portland suspended Wentworth's salary and refused to release it until he had accounted for all expenditures,"[409] a move which compounded the Lieutenant-Governor's already complicated personal finances.

By 21 December 1799 George Ross, "employed by the Directors of the Sierra Leone Company to attend the Maroons to that country," had arrived in Nova Scotia from Quebec where he had been with the ill-fated *Asia.* Ross, "obviously from Edenburg," was a product of the highly-rated Scottish school system, but perhaps not its brightest star. Campbell maintains that his journal was "just barely literate, clumsy for the most part, and with no claim to elegance of style," but that he was "obviously fairly well read." He began service as a clerk with the Sierra Leone Company on 10 December 1795. In 1797 he was made cashier, a position he at first refused due to the risk to health in the territory referred to as the "white man's grave," and due to the fact that he considered the salary of £100 insufficient to "furnish him decently with the bare demands of life." However, the governor and council convinced him to accept the post and in 1800 he was appointed Alderman under the new charter of the colony of the Sierra Leone Company.[410]

A meticulous compiler of trade records, and apparently lacking an inflated sense of his own importance, Ross must have been a trusted member of the Company when he was charged with the responsibility of conducting the Maroons from Nova Scotia to Sierra Leone. On his arrival in Halifax he first met with Wentworth, then went to Preston and visited the other Maroon communities. By January 1800 he had taken up residence at Maroon Hall and endeavoured "to learn their dispositions, and give them good impressions of the Country, whereto he is to attend them."[411] He was also responsible for ensuring that the Maroons were aware of the rules and conditions of settlement that the Sierra Leone Company had stipulated.

These, Wentworth suggested, they did not entirely approve of, although they were "satisfied to go to Africa."[412] Perhaps cynically, he commented that any agreement the Maroons might make would be "more in compliance with the requisition, than from any expectation of their being Bound thereby, or conformed thereto, further than they can evade, or resist."[413] Wentworth also stated that the "true radical cause why they refuse to sign the terms" was that they felt that Jamaica was "bound to maintain them without labour" and in Sierra Leone "they might gain possession of Slaves, women and labourers, by their own valour."[414]

Wentworth likely informed Ross of "the character and dispositions" of the Maroons and repeated to him his earlier warnings to Portland:

> [S]even or eight Families are particularly proud, truculent and savage. All the Men and youth will require great cir-

cumspection, vigilance and power to govern them in that climate, whence, they will be no better disposed to earn their own subsistence than in Nova Scotia. The greatest care must be taken to prevent their intercourse with slave traders, or other adventurers of any nation or language whatsoever, nor may they be entrusted with military Arms or ammunition or weapons of any sort — They already count upon their prowess in that Country.[415]

Wentworth especially complained of the difficulties he had with five families, "viz. 2 Jarratts, 2 Shaws, and Harding," who "have saved more money than the rest, and are the worst disposed." Wentworth warned that if they did not soon become "tired of their folly ... I shall probably send these five — to five remote towns in the Province, from whence they cannot depart." The records do not reveal whether Wentworth carried out his threat.[416] Ross, however, had the opportunity to form his own opinions about the Maroons, individually and collectively,[417] and by 10 June 1800,[418] on his return from a visit to the United States, he was ready for the voyage to Africa. In Nova Scotia Ross fulfilled his responsibilities competently and without annoying anyone, at least not to the point of warranting official complaints. Further, his journal reveals that on board the *Asia* and in Sierra Leone, he was a fairly tolerant and reasonably fair observer of the Maroon community.

Meanwhile, life went on in Halifax. The population had grown to over 8,500 living in 1,000 dwellings. The city's status was about to be confirmed with the construction of Government House, Nova Scotia's first major public works project of the nineteenth century. The house was purpose-built as the official residence of the lieutenant-governor, and remains so to the present day.

The Maroons contributed to the construction of this public monument on the eve of their departure from Halifax, just as they had to the Citadel on their arrival. "Maroons and soldiers were employed in the early stages, when there was digging and blasting to be done. The

Maroons ... came over from Preston under the watchful eye of Theophilus Chamberlain. The bill which Chamberlain presented in June 1800, shows that 'Sundry' Maroons had worked for 223 1/4 days at the rate of fifty shillings for twenty-five days."[419] It is paradoxical, but somehow appropriate that, as the Maroons awaited departure, their final contribution to Nova Scotia was as builders rather than as warriors.[420] By the time the cornerstone was laid, however, in September 1800, the Maroons were gone. So too was Prince Edward who in August 1800 was finally allowed, by his father, King George III, to go home.

While Ross, Wentworth and most of the Maroons were prepared for their embarkation, the *Asia* was not. On 31 May 1800 the ship finally arrived in Halifax from Quebec "having been assisted by some Pilots and other Men engaged for that passage only." Consequently, on 1 June 1800 "the *Asia* was twenty men short of her chartered complement, and continued so for some time." It proved to be difficult to hire seamen to undertake the voyage "altho' great wages and bounty were offered," and the *Asia* rode at anchor, the Maroons marked time, and both Ross and Wentworth fussed with the details of the migration.[421] On 6 June 1800 Wentworth enquired when the *Asia* would "be prepared to receive the Maroons on board, and proceed to sea,"[422] and on 10 June assured the Duke of Portland "of the perfect readiness of the Maroons, were and continues to be in, to be embarked at any moment when the *Asia* is manned, and otherwise prepared to receive them, to proceed to Africa."[423] Meanwhile, Wentworth continued to involve himself in the affairs of the Maroons by ordering a survey of provisions, especially the supply and quality of bread, on the *Asia*.[424] Not learning the lesson of the tobacco and brandy, he had supplied "some medicines, tea, sugar, wine and molasses for the use of the sick and aged people ... none being on board, and being probably accidentally omitted."[425]

CHAPTER 11

Migration to Sierra Leone: New Home or New Exile

Finally, on 28 July Wentworth was able to report that the Duke of Kent had engaged about forty discharged sailors. [426] This ad hoc crew was "to be embarked on board, to aid and assist in navigating and protecting the ship to Sierra Leone."[427] While the departure was again slightly delayed, embarkation was set for the twenty-eighth, with 2 August determined to be the day of departure "under convoy or in company with the Assistance Man of War, so far as to the Western Islands."[428] The "sundry stores, Implements of Husbandry and Clothing and Furniture … the property and for the use" of the Maroons were stowed away,[429] except for a "Part of the Necessaries to each Family and their Blankets and bedding for use on the Passage, and to be in their own care."[430] While some had been "careless of their tools, and implements, and clandestinely sold some," Wentworth was confident that they had enough to last them for three years in their new home.

Finally, on 3 August 1800 the *Asia* received on board "Five hundred and fifty one persons, in good health except three who are ill, and the infirmities natural to old age"[431] and Palmer's dog.[432] The Maroons, almost a year late, were ready to depart.

While they had not signed the terms proposed to them by Mr. Ross they had "amply and before many witnesses acceded to the terms, verbally."[433] However, Sir John complained, "Four have deserted to avoid going to Sierra Leone," so there was no absolute unanimity on the migration to Africa. While Wentworth reported that "the strictest search is making for them, if possible to discover and get them on board the ship," there is no indication if this effort was successful or if these four remained to help perpetuate the memory of the Maroons in Nova Scotia.[434] Winks observes:

The Maroons were by no means as badly off in terms of material possessions as the Nova Scotians, who had voluntarily preceded them. Major John Jarrett, his wife, and one of his daughters, for example, owned two coats, four vests, one pair of trousers, six shirts, four pairs of stockings, three pairs of shoes, two hats, twenty-four handkerchiefs, three walking sticks, sixteen gowns, fifteen petticoats, ten shifts, two women's hats, an apron, two towels, a tablecloth, a box of trinkets, twenty-one blankets, and miscellaneous bedding. There were three other Jarrett children, all presumably provided for in much the same way. Such entries are typical. Of the 550 Maroons recorded on the return (one seems to have escaped the census), there are 151 men, 177 women, and 222 children. [435]

With the final preparations made, the *Asia* prepared to depart. On 6 August 1800 Wentworth reported, "If the wind permits they will sail tomorrow,"[436] and either on 7 August, or more likely 8 August 1800, the Maroons sailed out of Nova Scotian history.[437] While he cautioned the Sierra Leone Company, Wentworth did not place the blame on the failed settlement effort in Nova Scotia on the Maroons themselves. Instead he pointed his finger at "those who led their minds astray, by petitions, advice, and other interferences,"[438] at "factious, self interested people"[439] and "interested insidious Men,"[440] who made "poisonous impressions … on their minds."[441] It was they, he insisted, that turned "these deluded people … from this situation of Health, Comfort, and prosperity, in sanguine expectations of savage enjoyments,"[442] and had convinced them "of the facility of conquest, which might supply their wants, and gratify their warlike, predatory, ambitious habits."[443] The extremes of this outside interference, Wentworth felt, had likely been limited by the "Maroons themselves, who, I am convinced, declined from violences, that were Suggested to them, as the means of obtaining a removal."[444]

If Wentworth's view is interpreted as that the Maroons did not know

their own minds, he was no doubt wrong and "his paternalistic insistence upon attending to the Maroons needs over their own leaders'
wishes … was ill-calculated to placate so vigorous a body."[445] While he
might be condemned for apparently being convinced that he always
knew what was best for them, Wentworth was, in Winks' assessment,

> a genuine friend to the Maroons in Nova Scotia. He had
> risked much on their behalf, for Portland was a powerful
> man, a necessary reinforcement to Pitt during his first
> administration. Wentworth had no wish to attract the
> enmity of the Portland Whigs, for he was too wise in the
> ways of political machination to misconceive his own rela-
> tively flimsy basis of power. Yet he persisted in the face of
> Portland, the Preston Maroons, and many in the white
> Nova Scotia community, to champion what he thought was
> the Maroons' cause.[446]

As the Maroons prepared to leave Nova Scotia, Wentworth's own
feelings might be contained in his comment, "I know not whether to
lament that my hopes of their civilization is not to be perfected here,
when the progress justified zeal and exertion or to indulge my charity
with wishes, that they may be made the instruments of conveying the
light and knowledge they have acquired, into the populous Regions
they are going to."[447] Wentworth's concern that the Maroons "in Sierra
Leone or some other climate, [other than Nova Scotia] … might gain
possession of slaves, women and labourers by their own valour"[448]
rather than farm for a living, was underscored when they, at the last
minute, "offered to send five hundred slaves back to Nova Scotia from
West Africa to replace their lost labour."[449]

The voyage of the Maroons to "the populous Regions" of Sierra
Leone in western Africa was eventful. The *Asia*, described as "a good
sailing ship,"[450] reached Freetown on 30 September 1800 and prepared
to land the following day. During the voyage the Maroons had complained that they had not received their full allotment of rations and

that grog had replaced the Jamaican rum that they had expected. Eventually it was discovered that the Maroons "were defrauded of some of their bread and ... [that] some of their provisions were actually sold for profits in Halifax even before they left Nova Scotia."[451]

Maroon complaints to Lieutenant John Sheriff, Master of the *Asia*; to George Ross,[452] their superintendent; and to Lieutenant Lionel Smith of the 24th Regiment of Foot, gradually bore fruit and the captain's steward, a Maroon, was dismissed from office and replaced by Maroon Captain Smith, who had served as "Issuer of Provisions and stores ..." at Maroon Town.[453] A much more satisfying part of the voyage was the mid-Atlantic encounter and capture of the Spanish ship, *El Angel*, and the subsequent sharing of the prize with all on board the *Asia*, including the Maroons. Lieutenant Lionel Smith agreed to act as Agent for the Maroons to collect their prize money which they applied to receive "in kind" after their settlement in Sierra Leone.[454]

Both James Palmer, the noted warrior of the Trelawny Town rebellion and leader of the Boydville Maroons, and his dog survived the trans-Atlantic voyage and disembarked in Freetown. Palmer's dog, however, became the first casualty of life in their new west African home. George Ross noted in his journal on 15 October 1800, "Poor Palmer's Dog: And Poor Palmer — after giving his poor dog a part of his own allowance all the way from Nova Scotia to be the very first night after landing devoured by a ravenous leopard!"[455]

Montague James also survived the crossing. He remained "greatly esteemed in Sierra Leone." When elderly he was among the first, if not the first, Sierra Leonian to receive an old age pension, which was granted to him by special order of the government, "to relieve the infirmities of his old age, and declining state of health." An even more significant honour made him a one-man "provisional government to execute the office of Governor and Council" of Sierra Leone during a short period when the Governor was out of the colony. This singular honour, perhaps the highest office that a black man held to that time in the British Empire, marked the zenith of his public career. His death likely occurred in 1811 or 1812.[456]

When the Maroons, together with the forty-seven officers and men of the 24th Regiment, arrived in Sierra Leone the colony was in a state of rebellion. A minority (but likely supported by the majority) of the Nova Scotian black loyalist settlers of 1792 was in conflict with the Sierra Leone Company that ran the colony and had drawn up a "settler constitution" which historian James Walker contends "was a declaration of Nova Scotian independence from the company government."[457] The armed stalemate which ensued was altered by the arrival of the *Asia* when, with the members of the 24th Regiment, "some 150 Maroon men, anxious to stretch their legs after a trans-Atlantic confinement and four years of inactivity in Nova Scotia, volunteered their services to the government."[458]

Robinson writes, "[T]he Trelawnys were thrown into the fight and helped to crush the rising. Everyone was suitably impressed by their warlike skill, and it was evident that the years spent in Nova Scotia, playing cards, lounging about and occasionally cultivating the land had not weakened their powers."[459] While this intervention did little to endear the Maroons to the Nova Scotian black loyalists,[460] it secured their welcome to official Sierra Leone and earned them a place in Sierra Leonian history.[461]

In Sierra Leone, they perpetuated the memory of their Jamaican home by the creation of Trelawny Street in Freetown, and it was reported that they

> universally harbour a desire of going back, at some period in their lives, to Jamaica, and therefore may with more difficulty be induced ... to labour for the improvement of their habitations or plantations. These circumstances render them a people not easy to be governed, and to be brought into that state of society which would best promote the civilization of Africa.[462]

CHAPTER 12

Balancing the Books

With the future of the Maroons now relegated to other hands, it was left to Wentworth to conclude the financial affairs of their past in Nova Scotia. Originally, accounts and vouchers were authorized by the Maroon superintendents, then, after he assumed control, approved by the lieutenant-governor, audited by the Council and sent to the Government of Jamaica and to the Home Secretary, who was the final authority that ultimately had to be satisfied. In 1799 Wentworth's situation was made more complicated in that "the clerk who has the charge of the Maroon Accounts is ordered for a short time on duty to Cape Breton,"[463] and later the clerk then in charge of the Maroon accounts died and the papers "detained" by his estate, "without which the public accounts he acted in cannot be easily perfected."[464]

Once the decision was made to sponsor the migration of the Maroons to Sierra Leone the "Estates and property of all descriptions" were ordered sold, but due to the delay of the *Asia* and Wentworth's admonition that "the estates cannot be sold, until the people are gone," there was little effort to dispose of the property until the fall of 1800.[465] This delay was likely providential as "so great is the scarcity of cash — That the Pay Master General who is also Agent for my Regt. has not been able to procure money to pay our Muster regularly for several months past."[466] While Wentworth assured Portland that the "completing and closing of the Maroon Accounts [would] be diligently and faithfully attended to,"[467] it was years before the books were finally balanced.

However, in the fall of 1800 and the spring of 1801 the records of the sales and auctions of the Maroon property testify to the great variety of items that were involved. Reverend Benjamin Gerrish Gray purchased a "Red Horse Call'd Brinley"; while Mr. Floyer [Fleigher?] bought a chestnut horse named, by some coincidence, Floyer; and a Mr. Halfpenny acquired a "Small Gray Horse with One Eye." Other purchasers obtained sheep, oxen, wheels, pitch forks, hoes, crow bars, candles, scythes, chains and even a "Broken Kettle."[468] Lands in Dartmouth, Lake Loon, Beaver Bank, Boydville, Preston, Chezzetcook, Cole Harbour Road and Windsor Road were all sold at public auction. Maroon Hall was purchased by Samuel Hart and the Boydville Farm by J. Lawlor, while other property, amounting to several thousand acres, were acquired by a variety of persons, although the sale of the Maroon Wharf "so called" had to be rescinded as it was "not Disposable being private property."

Meanwhile, the regular bills pertaining to the Maroons were still being processed. New sails for the Maroon boat had been purchased in the spring of 1800 and the bill for the "allowance for the Maroon Road through Cochrans Land across his Field" had been received. Lawrence Hartshorne, "agent for the removal of the Maroons," had to pay for the "25 tons of rice and 6 months provisions for food including flour and corn" that he had supplied.[469] In addition, bills for food, hay, cartage, legal fees, and the services of the surgeon, chaplain, and superintendent were recorded. Additional costs were accrued by advertising the sale of the Maroon lands, supplying punch for the sales, and for workmen "taking charge of the Property at Boydville, securing the windows of the Houses, [and] preserving the buildings and fences from Depredations." Another, perhaps revealing, notation was a bill for two copies of Goldsmith's *History of England*, five copperplate copy books, and one dictionary that had been "omitted from 8 Aug. 1800 for the Maroon Boys when embarked for Sierra Leone,"[470] evidence of Wentworth's ongoing interest in the "scholars" at the Maroon school.

None of this, however, was handled quickly. In April 1801 Wentworth promised that "the remainder of these last accounts will be completed as soon as possible."[471] He was extremely anxious to settle these accounts and hoped that any whiff of scandal that might have touched his over-expenditure on the Maroons, on defence, or on his new official residence, would be quickly forgotten. Indeed, their persistence "had led Wentworth to fear in 1801-2 that he might be demoted to a West Indian post."[472] However, in June 1804, the Maroon accounts were still not settled as Wentworth explained to the Lords Commissioners of the Treasury:

> The final arrangement of the Maroon accounts has been delayed by the difficulties attending the sales of such various and extensive property — at a time when circulating monies in the Province was much reduced; and since those sales — by the sickness and death of the late James Clark Esq. who was Clerk and accountant for that department, and of course had all the papers relative thereto in his Custody, which, after his decease was detained by his Estate — but having lately delivered them to me. The Accounts now settled a balance due to me — will next week be proved, examined and audited by his Majesty's Council, and immediately afterwards transmitted to your Lordships, I trust they will be found correctly right, as the greatest care is exercised to have them so, and they will be finally approved. [473]

While Wentworth was not to be embarrassed by demotion, his long sought-after promotion to the position of Governor-General of British North America did not materialize. Despite the best efforts of Earl Fitzwilliam, the nephew of the Marquis of Rockingham, and the "steadfast support of the Duke of Kent, who pressed Wentworth's case" Wentworth's star had already reached its zenith.[474]

Indeed, Sir John did not live long enough to see the final judgement on the Maroon accounts. Although he survived until 1820, the "accounts were finally certified as correct eight months after his death. The balance due Wentworth was £8,864" and was likely paid to Wentworth's son, Charles Mary.[475] The accounts reveal that the Maroon experiment was expensive. It cost the Jamaican government "upwards of forty six thousand pounds,"[476] while "ultimately the transfer and attendant expenses were to cost the British government over £60,000."[477] It cost Wentworth financial difficulties for years and threatened both his position and the security of his family within the hierarchy of the imperium. [478]

Conclusion

The question that remains is whether the Maroons are really worthy of note, or are they simply a footnote in the history of eighteenth-century Nova Scotia. Their sojourn in the province was, after all, only four years and their final year was one of waiting to leave and so can be largely dismissed as "marking time." While reference to Maroon Hall, the Maroon Bastion and to Maroon Hill have helped to perpetuate their memory in the Halifax area, the bastion did not long outlast them, their connection to the place name was largely unheralded, and the "only place where the name Maroon Hall is preserved . . .[is] in Christ Church Cemetery" on a headstone.[479] Moreover, while their reputation was based on their military prowess, any contribution they might have made in the face of a French invasion of the province was, of course, negated because the French did not invade. Obviously, then, their ongoing impact on Nova Scotia was not military.

Economically, the arrival and continued presence of the Maroons was of at least local significance. While many of the provisions for the Maroons were purchased in London and New York, there is no doubt that Halifax-Dartmouth merchants also benefitted. The sale of lands in Preston, Dartmouth, and "on the Windsor Road" was of immediate bounty to the conveyors and simultaneously injected more money into the local economy. Their presence also resulted in road construction (Ochterloney St. was the beginning of Highway 7), and the maintenance of the "Maroon Establishment" likewise contributed to the stimulation of the local economy. As a source of business and as a supply of labour the Maroons were no doubt of short-term importance, and this influence ended when the Maroons emigrated. Accordingly, it would be hard to argue that the Maroons had any long-term economic significance.

In terms of local politics it would also be difficult to argue for the importance of the Maroons. While their affairs no doubt occupied more of Lieutenant-Governor Wentworth's time than any other group of similar size in the colony, and they were a catalyst in the Wentworth-Tonge constitutional debate, as well as landing Wentworth in a world of trouble with his superiors in London, his hopes were dashed when they left. His time and his trouble were the price that he paid for his failure to convince the Maroons that Nova Scotia was their home. Their direct influence on Wentworth and local affairs ended not long after their emigration.

It is also difficult to determine what influence or affect the Maroons had on the established African Nova Scotian community. Little is revealed in the official records but no doubt there was interaction between the Maroons, the black loyalists, and the local slave population. There was, at least, one planned marriage between a Maroon man and a Nova Scotian "woman of a good Carth [character], she is a nitive [native] of this Country" who could spin, sew, and cook.[480] While prejudice would likely preclude this reference being to other than an African Nova Scotian woman, we do not know if the marriage in fact took place or if she migrated to Sierra Leone. In the face of this slim evidence, it would likely be precipitous to suggest that the Maroons had great immediate influence on black Nova Scotia. Nor do we know whether the Maroons had meaningful contact or connection with the Mi'kmaq of the area. While the listing of "1 Indian Box" among the possessions of the Andrew Smith family might suggest a link, it is equally possible that the box was a casual purchase at the Halifax market or elsewhere.[481]

On a larger stage the Maroons present the student of history with a study in inter-colonial and imperial relations. Jamaica was a wealthier and thus, in imperial eyes, a much more important colony than Nova Scotia. However, the Maroons presented much more than an interaction between these two colonies. Obviously, Britain was also involved with both in the interests of each and with concern for the Maroons themselves, if only because of the political implications for an unstable government. Similarly, the African homeland colony of Sierra Leone was involved as a player in this increasingly many sided picture. Thus Jamaica politics, Nova Scotia politics, British politics, and Sierra Leonian politics were intertwined. Likewise political pressure, pressure groups, and, fundamentally, the exercise of power were involved. A fascinating picture, but one in which the Maroons, while nominally the lead actors, were really little more than bit players in the larger drama. The historian must also be careful to note that while many of the Maroons were anxious to leave Nova Scotia, Jamaica rather than Africa would have been their destination of first choice. It is, therefore, difficult to read this migration as part of a "back to Africa" movement. Equally difficult to assess, from this perspective, is the importance of the Nova Scotian experience to the Maroons themselves. While the turn of this century, with its full complement of displaced persons, has made the study of the impact of displacement on the displaced an important topic, it was not much, if at all, considered two hundred years ago. Moreover, the Maroons were in Nova Scotia for such a short time that, unlike the black loyalist emigrants to Sierra Leone and the white Scottish St. Ann's emigrants to New Zealand, their descendants are unlikely to refer to themselves as Nova Scotians.

Perhaps the most real, long-lasting influence of the Maroons is the one that is the most difficult to measure. The bloodlines of the Maroons may have long since run thin in Nova Scotia, but the spirit of the Maroons has survived. This spirit is their legacy to the Nova Scotian black community. Like the Highlanders of Scotland, the real or spiritual ancestors of many white Nova Scotians whose collective memory is stirred by the vision of kilted warriors pouring out of their hills, their banners flying, their pipes bawling, and their claymores flashing in the sun, to avenge some real or imagined insult, or to rally for some lost cause, the Maroons represent the indomitable pride of being to many black Nova Scotians. The Maroons, like the Scottish Highlanders, possessed characteristics that we might not always want our children to emulate, but in time of need they are the spiritual ancestors who recall group pride, the inner sense of dignity, the cohesion, and the strength that can provide a people with the will to carry on. This, perhaps, is the historical importance of the Maroons to Nova Scotia and this is why we should remember them.

ENDNOTES

Chapter 1

1. Brymner, p. 84.
2. Robinson, *Fighting*, p. 10.
3. Governor's Letter Book, vol. 52, p. 229. Letter, Sir John Wentworth to Richard Moleworth, 17 November 1798.
4. Augier p. 17.
5. Robinson, *Fighting*, p. 12.
6. Ibid., p. 14. Robinson states that the Arawaks "once about 60,000 strong, had almost disappeared by 1611."
7. Ibid., p. 16.
8. Augier, p. 49.
9. Robinson, *Fighting*, p. 17.
10. Sheehan, p. 9.
11. Patterson, p. 263.
12. Brymner, p. 81.
13. Higman, p. 386.
14. Augier, p. 109.
15. Patterson, p. 249.
16. Simons, p. 9.
17. Augier, p. 88. See also Campbell, *Maroons*, *passim*.
18. Patterson, p. 246. In this paper Patterson presents his hypothesis that "large-scale, monopolistic slave systems with a high rate of absenteeism will, with geographic conditions permitting, exhibit a high tendency toward slave revolts" (p. 289), and his argument that Jamaica fulfilled all these conditions.
19. Robinson, *Fighting*, p. 51.
20. Augier, p. 88.
21. Campbell, "Early Resistance," p. 89.
22. Campbell, *Maroons*, pp. 196-7; Robinson, *Fighting*, p. 74 and *passim*.
23. Genovese, p. 67.
24. Campbell, *Maroons*, pp. 222-3.
25. Ibid., p. 211; Robinson, *Fighting*, p. 82.
26. Genovese, p. 67.
27. Figures estimate 25,000 whites, 250,000 slaves, and 32,000 "coloured." In addition, there were approximately 10,000 Free Blacks, including the Maroons.Craton, p. 275. This ratio had developed earlier. In Jamaica as early as 1713, "the slaves outnumbered their masters by eight to one . . . in Jamaica a small cadre of white masters was nakedly pitted against their black slaves." Dunn, p. 165.
28. Augier, p. 114.
29. Cundall, p. 327.
30. One colourful account has Balcarres only slightly wounded even after thirteen bullets passed through his clothing, and having to surrender at Ticonderoga in 1777. He was held prisoner until 1779.
31. Robinson, *Fighting*, p. 90. Accompong was another Maroon Town in Jamaica. Campbell's chapter, "The Trelawny Town War, 1795-1796," provides an excellent account of the engagement. *Maroons*, pp. 207-49.
32. Sheehan, p. 8.
33. Campbell, "Early Resistance," pp. 93-4.
34. Winks, p. 79.
35. Cundall, p. 329.
36. Winks, p. 79. See Philalethes for an account of this practice.

37. Winks, p. 79, writes "offered" a truce. Robinson, *Fighting*, pp. 129-30 writes that while historians suggest the Maroons proposed the terms, "this seems extremely unlikely, since it was the troops who had come seeking peace."

38. Robinson, *Fighting*, p. 130.

39. Ibid., p. 133.

40. Campbell, *Maroons*, p. 235.

41. Winks, p. 80.

42. Campbell, *Maroons*, p. 239..

43. In his later years Balcarres wrote "Anecdotes of a Soldier's Life" and completed "Memoirs of the Lindsays," which had been started by his father. Balcarres had four sons and two daughters.

44. Robinson, *Fighting*, pp. 137-40.

45. Campbell, *Maroons*, p. 242. William Dunlap reported a conversation with Alexander Ochterlony in Boston in December 1797. He wrote that Smith, "who was employed to persuade his countrymen to comply with the wishes of the legislature, under promise of liberty to return," was detained in Nova Scotia "contrary to the wishes of the commissioners." *Diary of William Dunlop*, vol. 1, p. 186.

46. Campbell, "Early Resistance," p. 96.

47. Campbell, *Maroons*, pp. 237-8, 241. Abraham D. Dridzo, p. 21, has advanced another thesis on the cause of the Maroon War of 1795-1796. He argues that "the rising of the Maroons in 1795 was provoked by an influential group of Jamaican planters." This conspiracy of wealth "was brought about in order to influence the internal policies of Great Britain, to deflect that policy and thus advance the interests of the Jamaican planters."

48. 28 July 1796.

49. Throne, p. 474. See also Lee, vol. 59, "Walpole."

50. For a discussion of "who then, was responsible for sending the Maroons to Nova Scotia?" see Campbell, *Nova Scotia*, pp. 12-3.

51. Colonial Office Records (CO), vol. 67, Letter, Governor A. Lindsay, Lord Balcarres of Jamaica, to Wentworth, 3 June 1796.

52. Winks, p. 80. See also Note 51.

53. Campbell, *Nova Scotia*, p. 251, n. 2, notes, "Their slaves were expected to be sold by the Jamaican government before their deportation."

54. Campbell, *Maroons*, p. 241.

55. T.C. Haliburton, vol. 2, p. 285. This list corresponds with Robinson and others. However, Edward Augustus identified the carriers as "the *Dover*, forty-four, and two transports." Letter Book of Prince Edward, Letter #255, Prince Edward to the Duke of Portland, 15 August 1796.

Chapter 2

56. CO, vol. 67, Letter, Dr. J. Oxley to Wentworth, 16 June 1798.

57. Robinson, *Fighting*, p. 143.

58. Dallas and Brymner state 21 and 23 July as dates of arrival. These dates correspond with those given by Winks, Robinson, and others. Picart states that they arrived on 22 and 23 July, *Collections*, p. 172. However, in a letter to the Duke of Portland on 23 July 1796 Wentworth stated that he was sending a copy of the letter from Balcarres, "which I received yesterday, by Mr. Quarrell, who arrived in the *Dover* Transport, the other Transport arrived the 21 instant," Governor's Letter Book, vol. 51, p. 330. See also the letter from Oxley to Wentworth, 16 June

1798, in which he states that he arrived in Nova Scotia with the Maroons on 22 July 1796, CO, vol. 69. For further evidence supporting 21 and 22 July 1796, see Campbell, *Nova Scotia*, p. 16.

59. Brymner says 543 (p. 83). Archibald, "Story of Deportation," gives the number between 500 and 600 (p. 150). T.C. Haliburton says they amounted to 600 (vol. 2, p. 285). Winks specifies 556 as the number boarded in Jamaica (p. 80). Picart gives 563 as the number. In *Maroons*, Campbell says that 568 were boarded (p. 241). If Robinson's figure of 17 deaths is correct, then 551, plus any births, should have arrived in Halifax. In a 13 June 1796 letter from Portland, Wentworth was warned to expect from eight to nine hundred, but this was clearly incorrect, CO, vol. 67.

60. Letter Book of Prince Edward, Letter #260, Prince Edward to Colonel Brownrigg, 15 August 1796.

61. Winks, p. 81. Edward Augustus, one of the soldier sons of King George III, had arrived in Halifax in May 1794 as general officer commanding the district.

62. Bryan Edwards, p. xxxix. In *Nova Scotia*, p. 256, n. 25, Campbell describes Edwards as "an implacable enemy of the Maroons," as attested to by his writing. The Maroons were apparently aware of Edwards' work. Andrew Smith, Captain of the Maroons, stated: "Ask Masa Bryan Edwards if him no shame to tell lye so." Smith castigated the honesty and honour of Edwards' entire family, concluding, "O Bad family, true true." See also Andrew Smith's 3 June 1797 letter to his brother Charles Samuels, CO, vol. 69; and Campbell, *Nova Scotia*, p. 60, for a translation of the Maroon Creole of the document.

63. Winks, p. 80.

64. Robinson, *Fighting*, p. 145. See also Dallas, v. 2. pp. 206-9. The height and size of the Maroons is further attested to by the order for "sundry articles" for the Maroons, including 150 great coats "to be made large, and about 50 very long " the remainder usual lengths" and "50 doz. Strong good Shoes, some to be the largest sizes, sorted down to children of 7 years old "with leather shoe strings," CO, vol. 67, "Memorandums of Sundry Articles required to be imported from England for the use of the Maroons," 13 August, 1796.

65. Letter Book of Prince Edward, Letter #260, Prince Edward to Brownrigg, 15 August 1796.

66. CO, vol. 67, #17. Portland had also been in error about the number to be sent. William Henry Cavendish-Bentinck (1738-1809), the third Duke of Portland had a long career in politics. He held various important offices including that of Prime Minister. He was Home Secretary (1794-1801) which included responsibility for the colonies.

67. Ibid., #18.

68. *Weekly Chronicle*, 23 July 1796.

69. Robinson, *Fighting*, p. 144. See also Dallas, vol. 2, p. 485, and Thomas Barclay to Wentworth, 25 May 1799 CO, vol. 70. In his letter Barclay, Speaker of the Nova Scotia House of Assembly (1793-1799) and a personal friend of Wentworth's, stated that he was one who had advised Wentworth not to allow the Maroons to stay in Nova Scotia but had been convinced otherwise. In 1799 Barclay returned to his native New York with the appointment as the British Consul-General to the Northern and Eastern States of America. Michael Wallace, MHA for Halifax County, also reported himself convinced by Quarrell that the Maroons would be peaceful and useful settlers, CO, vol. 70, Letter, Wallace to Wentworth, 15 July 1799.

70. Governor's Letter Book, vol. 51, p. 330, Letter, Wentworth to Portland, 23 July, 1796.

71. Akins, p. 112. In 1796 the Contre Amiral Joseph de Richery (1757-1799) wrought havoc in the fishing fleet and captured or sank 80 vessels.
72. Letter Book of Prince Edward, Letter, Prince Edward to the Duke of York, 10 September 1794.
73. Cuthbertson, *The Loyalist Governor*, p. 76.
74. J. Plimsoll Edwards, p. 77.
75. "The exodus, which took place in January 1792, had the economic effect that had been feared by the province's employers and proprietors. Trade was depressed by the removal of so many black consumers and the province was deprived of "useful laborers." The new governor, John Wentworth, and several other dignitaries recorded their conviction that Nova Scotia had been seriously damaged by the departure of the major pool of available casual labor," Walker, "The Establishment of a Free Black Community," p. 223.
76. Letter Book of Prince Edward, Letter #255, Prince Edward to Portland, 15 August 1790.
77. Governor's Letter Book, vol. 51, p. 333, Letter, Wentworth to Portland, 13 August 1796.
78. Ibid., p. 332, Letter, Wentworth to Portland, 15 July 1796. This move fitted with Portland's suggestions recorded in a letter he wrote to Wentworth on 15 July 1796, C0, vol.67, #18. Campbell provides a wonderful review of the issue of whether the Maroons had offered to work on the Citadel for free. Her conclusion, to which I fully subscribe, is if they did "make such an offer it would have been dictated by diplomatic nicety," *Nova Scotia*, pp. 252-3, n. 14. It certainly would have not have been in character for them to expect less than the best received, as Alexander Howe asserted, "the Maroons will not work without pay *equal to a white man*," C0, vol. 69, Letter, Howe to Wentworth, Preston, 8 June 1798. In *The History of the Dartmouth Quakers*, Trider claims that "Wentworth's Preston estate was built largely at the expense of the free labour of the Maroons" (p. 132). While there were Maroons on the estate in the early days of their settlement, it is unlikely that Wentworth got much for free.
79. Piers, p. 24.

Chapter 3

80. Dallas, vol. 2, p. 210.
81. Winks, p. 81. Akins states that "some were accordingly accommodated within sheds, and others placed in barns and such places of shelter as could be found in the town for their temporary accommodation" (p. 112). Duncan Campbell writes that they "occupied wooden shanties and tents on the citadel ground" (p. 202).
82. Governor's Letter Book, vol. 51, p. 333, Letter, Wentworth to Portland, 13 August 1796.
83. Ibid., p. 330, Letter, Wentworth to Portland, 23 July 1796.
84. Winks, p. 81.
85. Letter Book of Prince Edward, Letter #255, Prince Edward to Portland, 15 August 1796.
86. Cuthbertson, *The Loyalist Governor, passim*; Fingard, pp. 429-30.
87. C0, vol. 70, Letter, Wentworth to Portland, 30 May 1799. This letter enclosed, "Statement of Facts representing the settling of Maroons in Nova Scotia, refered [*sic*] to by the Lieutenant Governor of that Province, 29 May 1799." See Campbell, *Nova Scotia*, p. 126.

88. Cuthbertson, *The Loyalist Governor*, p. 78.

89. Winks, p. 81.

90. His plan also complied with the initial request of Balcarres to allow Quarrell to buy some land for the Maroons in Nova Scotia or New Brunswick. See CO, vol. 67, Letter, Balcarres to Wentworth, 3 June 1796.

91. CO, vol. 67, #18.

92. Raddall, p. 122.

93. CO, vol. 70, "Statement of Facts." In Campbell, *Nova Scotia*, p. 126.

94. Governor's Letter Book, vol. 51, p. 333, Letter, Wentworth to Portland, 13 August 1796.

95. Cuthbertson, *The Loyalist Governor*, p. 80.

96. Governor's Letter Book, vol. 51, p. 333, Letter, Wentworth to Portland, 13 August 1796.

97. CO, vol. 67, Letter, William Scott to Portland, 8 September 1796.

98. Ibid., Letter, Portland to Wentworth, 7 September 1796.

99. Governor's Letter Book, vol. 51, p. 333, Letter, Wentworth to Portland, 13 August 1796.

100. See, for example, Governor's Letter Book, vol. 51, p. 313, Letter, Wentworth to Hammond, 16 August 1796.

101. CO, vol. 68, "Report on Maroon Health," Oxley to Wentworth, 31 May 1797.

102. Governor's Letter Book, vol. 51, p. 333, Letter, Wentworth to Portland, 13 August 1796.

103. Ibid., p. 313, Letter, Wentworth to Hammond, 16 August 1796.

104. Ibid. p. 357, #29, Letter, Wentworth to Portland, 20 September 1796.

105. CO, vol. 68, Letter, Wentworth to Portland, 21 December 1796.

106. Governor's Letter Book, vol. 51, #29, p. 357, Letter, Wentworth to Portland, 20 September 1796.

107. The supplies were still in London in September. A 27 September 1796 letter from Milligan & Mitchell to the Lord Commissioners of the Admiralty explained that they "provided every article, which are now ready to be shipt [*sic*], but find that at present there is but one vessel bound to that port, and being unarmed must sail with convoy," CO, vol. 67. For a list of the "Sundry Articles from England for the use of the Maroons," see Campbell, *Nova Scotia*, pp. 26-8.

108. Governor's Letter Book, vol. 51, p. 310, Letter, Wentworth to Milligan & Mitchell, 15 August 1796.

109. Ibid., p. 313, Letter, Wentworth to Hammond, 16 August 1796.

110. Robinson, *Fighting*, p. 146.

111. Governor's Letter Book, vol. 51, p. 347, Letter, Wentworth to Balcarres, 10 October 1796.

112. Dallas, vol. 2, p. 212.

113. Governor's Letter Book, vol. 51, p. 310, Letter, Wentworth to Milligan & Mitchell, 15 August 1796.

114. Dallas, vol. 2, p. 496.

115. Robinson, *Fighting*, p. 147. See also Dallas, vol. 2, p. 214. T.C. Haliburton, vol. 2, p. 289, states that Quarrell "had throughout disapproved of setting the Maroons in a body." Haliburton obviously agreed with Quarrell as he discounted "the absurd plan of settling the Maroons in a compact body in this Province" (p. 291). Picart, based on Robinson, reports that Quarrell was in favour of "dispersing them throughout the Maritimes" (p. 176).

116. Dallas, vol. 2, p. 214.

Chapter 4

117. Walker, "The Royal Mistresses," p. 19.
118. Fingard, p. 849.
119. Cuthbertson, *The Loyalist Governor*, p. 93; Raddall, p. 96.
120. McNutt, "Edward Augustus," p. 297.
121. Walker, "Royal Mistresses," p. 19.
122. Raddall, p. 126.
123. Governor's Letter Book, vol. 51, p. 9, Letter, Wentworth to Portland, 8 October 1796.
124. Cuthbertson, *The Loyalist Governor*, pp. 75-9 and *passim*.
125. Governor's Letter Book, vol. 52, p. 5, Letter, Wentworth to Stuart, Cutter, Nixon, 30 December 1796.
126. Governor's Letter Book, vol. 51, p. 341, Letter, Wentworth to Portland, 24 September 1796. "Bay of Bulls" is now called Bay Bulls, as in fact it was in 1796. See the description of Bay Bulls in the *Royal Gazette*, 20 December 1796, p. 2. It is located on the east coast of the Avalon Peninsula. It was one of the earliest English settlements in Newfoundland and that province's earliest known English place name. It was occupied during the 1630s and attacked by the French five times between 1696 and 1796. See McNutt, *The Atlantic Provinces*, p. 116.
127. Edwards, "Militia," p. 76. The Royal Nova Scotia Regiment, commanded by Colonel Sir John Wentworth, was raised in September 1792 and disbanded on 24 August 1802. See Head Quarters Office.
128. CO, vol. 69, Letter, Andrew Smith to Charles Samuels, 3 June 1797. On the advice of Quarrell, Wentworth commissioned, "as a reward of merit, specified Maroons as part of his plan to embody the Maroons as a military corps," Dallas, vol. 2, p. 501.
129. Governor's Letter Book, vol. 51, p. 357, Letter, Wentworth to Portland, 20 September 1796. Over two hundred years later the measure of "cruel proportion" is no doubt very different. In 1796, the *Halifax Journal* matter-of-factly reported on 3 November 1796, "Yesterday Myles O'Brien, who was tried last Supreme Court, for forgery, stood for one hour in the Pillory, and had one of his ears cut off, according to his sentence."
130. Campbell, *Back to Africa*, p. xvi.
131. Winks, p. 82.
132. CO, vol. 67, Memorandum, 13 August 1796. See also, Governor's Letter Book, Letters, vol. 51, Wentworth to Egerton, 15 August 1796, p. 311, and Wentworth to Milligan and Mitchell, 15 August 1796, p. 310.
133. Cuthbertson, *The Loyalist Governor*, p. 81. T.G. Roberts made the questionable assertion, "The adjutant-general of the provincial militia was somewhat embarrassed by His Excellency the Governor's generosity in the matter of rank for the dusky officers of the Maroon companies," "Magnificent Army Men". This article, like its companion pieces, likely appeared in *The Halifax Chronicle* between October and December 1942, or early in 1943. I have not found support for this assertion anywhere in the material available to me. It is doubly questionable as the Adjutant General, Benning Wentworth, was John Wentworth's brother-in-law. Arthur Silver also claimed that the new designations "flattered their [the Maroons?] vanity" and thereafter they "strutted about with insolent swagger . . . profoundly conscious of their newly acquired dignity" (p. 187).

Chapter 5

134. Edwards, "Observations."
135. Lawson, p. 172.
136. Governor's Letter Book, vol. 51, p. 347, Letter, Wentworth to Balcarres, 10 October 1796.
137. Ibid., p. 333, Letter, Wentworth to Portland, 13 August 1796.
138. CO, vol. 67, #21, Letter, Portland to Wentworth, 16 October 1796.
139. Governor's Letter Book vol. 51, p. 257, Letter, Wentworth to Portland, 20 September 1796. Gray had been ordained deacon in 1795. He was the son of wealthy pre-revolution American immigrants and had inherited considerable property in Nova Scotia from his uncle Benjamin Gerrish. He was admitted to holy orders in 1797.
140. Ibid., p. 347, Letter, Wentworth to Balcarres, 10 October 1796.
141. Gray received an additional £30 for the S.P.G. appointment. See Macleod, pp. 12-13. In 1799-1800 Gray was also the grand chaplain of the provincial grand lodge of the masonic order. With the departure of the Maroons, he became an English Master at Kings College School, Windsor, before accepting the foremost Church of England congregation in Saint John, New Brunswick where he had a distinguished career. See Young.
142. Gray later reported that his "arrival among them" was on 6 November 1796. See CO, vol. 69, Letter, Gray to Wentworth, Preston, 18 June 1798.
143. Governor's Letter Book, vol. 52, #31, p. 1, Letter, Wentworth to Portland, 21 December, 1796.
144. Lawson; Tratt, pp. 128-30. Theophilus Chamberlain was buried, at his own request, "atop a high hill in Preston" in the cemetery of the church built for the Maroons.
145. C0, vol. 68, Letter, Wentworth to Portland, 7 May 1797, in Campbell, *Nova Scotia*, p. 37.
146. CO, vol. 70, Letter, Wentworth to John King, 18 August 1799, in Campbell, *Nova Scotia*, p. 138-40. Wentworth seemed to consider King as a friend in court and they both had connections to the Rockinghams. As under secretary in the Home Department, King potentially had access to influence and power. See Nelson, pp. 33-6.
147. pp. xvii-xviii. This same view was expressed by Dallas, vol. 2, p. 449. Writing about the Maroons who stayed in Jamaica and advocating "the establishment of Christianity" among them, Dallas states, "These people, however averse themselves to any alterations of their customs, have no objectives to their children being brought up Christians."
148. CO, vol. 69, Letter, Gray to Wentworth, 18 June 1798.
149. Macleod, p. 13.
150. Governor's Letter Book, vol. 52, p. 283, Letter, Wentworth to Dr. Morice, 1 May 1799. Rev. Dr. W. Morice had been elected Secretary of the S.P.G. in 1798.
151. Martin, p. 95. Louis Philippe was King of France from 1830-1848, but the "Citizen King" died in England after the 1848 Revolution forced him back into exile.
152. See Campbell, *Back to Africa*, p. 13, for example.
153. Governor's Letter Book, vol. 52, #37, p. 1, Letter, Wentworth to Portland, 21 December 1796.
154. CO, vol. 69, Letter, Oxley to Wentworth, 16 June 1798.
155. Campbell, *Nova Scotia*, p. 207 states, "Their marriages were attended with no

religious or judicial ceremonies — simple consent being sufficient; plurality of wives was allowed, but few had more than two." Campbell also notes, "[W]hen a man made a present to one of his wives he was bound to make a similar one to the others. Each wife lived in turn with her husband two days, and the children of the different women were only noticed by the father on the days that the respective mothers lived with him."

156. T.C. Haliburton, vol. 2, p. 288.
157. CO, vol. 69, p. 116, Letter, Gray to Wentworth, 18 June 1798. See also T.C. Haliburton, vol. 2, p. 288, where he states, "But the difficulty of conveying instructions to them, on account of their ignorance of the English language, was such, that the delivery of a sermon was a mere form, rendered as disagreeable to the preacher as it was useless to the people, some of them amusing themselves with smoking, while others fell asleep from weariness."
158. Dallas, vol. 2, p. 226.
159. Picart, p. 174. In an 18 June 1798 letter sent to Wentworth, Gray explained, "They allow Polygamy; and they part with their interest in their wives only if compensation being made. It is known that the engagements we make in our Matrimonial Service, are directly opposite to these two practices," CO, vol. 69.
160. Walker, *Black Loyalists*, p. 341.
161. Vol. 2, p. 290. Haliburton is obviously dependent on Dallas for much of this information. For example, see Dallas, vol. 2, pp. 251-2 for comparison.
162. Picart, p. 175. See also Silver, p. 188.
163. Pigou, pp. 24-5.
164. Campbell, *Back to Africa*, pp. xiii-xiv.
165. Ibid.
166. Ibid., pp. 32, 28.
167. Winks, p. 83.
168. Bilby, "The Kromanti Dance," pp. 53, 55, 57, 71-75, 76-77. See also Bilby, "How the 'Older Heads' Talk," pp. 37-88.
169. Ibid.
170. Ibid.
171. Raddall, p. 122.
172. Hamilton, "The Africans in Canada," p. 7.
173. Campbell, *Nova Scotia*, p. 73.
174. CO, vol. 69, Letter (with enclosures), Wentworth to Portland, 23 June 1798.
175. Vernon, p. 227. The other inhabitants of the Windsor Road were also able to take advantage of Gray's presence.
176. p. 187.
177. Governor's Letter Book, vol. 52, p. 283, Letter, Wentworth to Dr. Morice, 1 May 1799. This church was built and was likely the original St. John's, which was destroyed by fire in 1828 and replaced by the present structure. See Grant, "The Origins of Maroon Hill," pp. 4-5. The parish church of Preston, consecrated 26 June 1792, was called St. John's-on-the-Hill. In 1796, without clergy and few adherents, "it seemed as if the parish and church of St. John's were to be no more"; but the arrival of the Maroons gave it "a new lease on life." With the departure of the Maroons, and of their Chaplain, "the parish ceased to function in 1801 and remained closed until 1817," MacLeod, pp. 4, 9, 11, 14. By 1890 there was in Sierra Leone "a Maroon church at Freetown called St. John's," which is at least an interesting coincidence. See Hamilton, "The Maroons of Jamaica," p. 10.
178. Pascoe, pp. 116-7.

179. Campbell, *Fighting Maroons*, p. 77.
180. p. 189. In the spring of 1998 an archeological assessment report was prepared on the investigation of stone mounds reported on property which bordered the Maroon Hill (Boydville) area. It was determined that the stone piles found in the proposed "Daytona Park" sub-division of Middle Sackville, N.S., "do not appear to have any function other than for the storage of stones: and "are not considered archaeologically significant," Sheldon, p. 8.
181. CO, vol. 69, p. 118, Letter, Gray to Wentworth, Preston, 18 June 1798.
182. Ibid., Letter, Wentworth to Portland, 20 September 1796.
183. Ibid, vol. 68, Letter, Wentworth to Portland, 7 May 1797, in Campbell, *Nova Scotia*, p. 37.
184. Governor's Letter Book, vol. 52, p. 283, Letter, Wentworth to Dr. Morice, 1 May 1799.
185. CO, vol. 70, "Statement of Facts." In Campbell, *Nova Scotia*, p. 124. The capitalization, etc., are Wentworth's.
186. Picart, p. 175. In his Master's thesis, and his article based on it, Picart presents an interesting discussion of the relationship of the Trelawny Maroons and Sir John Wentworth, contending that the Maroons' resistance to settlement in Nova Scotia was a struggle for cultural survival. Though perhaps his argument is sometimes weakened by being overstated (for example, if cultural survival was the goal why did the Maroons allow their children to go to school, etc.), it is an engaging account and the most recent discussion of the Maroons in Nova Scotia.

Chapter 6

187. Maroon Hall was a large summer house built in 1792 for Francis Green, the Sheriff of Halifax Co. It occupied part of the grounds of what is now Dartmouth Memorial Gardens. See Lawson, pp. 176-84, for an account of Maroon Hall from its construction to its destruction by fire in 1856. The main building was a 40'x40' two-storey structure. In the dispersement of the Maroon holdings, Maroon Hall was sold to Halifax merchant Samuel Hart for £655 on 8 October 1801. See *Report on the Provincial Museum*, p. 45.
188. In a letter to Portland on 2 June 1797, Wentworth described Oxley as "being a prudent, well disposed Man, eminent in his Profession, kindly attached to these People, and better acquainted with their Constitutions, Habits and Dispositions, than any other Man, and therefore is and can be peculiarly useful to them," CO, vol. 67.
189. It certainly took up a valuable part of Wentworth's time. He made reference to it on various occasions. In August he reported, "I visit them every day." In October he admitted, "it will continue to be a source of increased care and attention to me," Governor's Letter Book, vol. 51, pp. 313, 357, Letter, Wentworth to Hammond, 16 August 1796, and Letter, Wentworth to Portland, 29 October 1796.
190. CO, vol. 67, Letter, Wentworth to Portland, 29 October 1796.
191. Ibid., #23, Letter, Portland to Wentworth, 14 December 1796.
192. See CO, vol. 68, Letter, Oxley to Wentworth, Maroon Town, 31 May 1797, in which he pronounced "them as healthy as any set of people on Earth."
193. CO, vol. 68, Letter, Howe to Quarrell, 9 August 1797.
194. *Columbian Centinel*, 16 December 1797, p. 1. Letter from "Humanitus" to B. Russell, Halifax, July 1797.
195. Dallas, vol. 2, p. 488.
196. Governor's Letter Book, vol. 52, #41, p. 53.

197. CO, vol. 69, Letter, Gray to Wentworth, 18 June 1798. The punctuation, spelling etc., are Gray's. A stove in a church was, apparently, a novel concept in Nova Scotia. Raddall comments, "Until this time the churches had been heated chiefly by the warmth of piety" (p. 126). A stoves was installed in St. Andrew's in 1795 and in St. Paul's in 1796.
198. Governor's Letter Book, vol. 52, #44, p. 65, Letter, Wentworth to Portland. See also Ibid., p. 36, Letter, Wentworth to Duke of Clarence, 21 April 1797. In this letter Wentworth admitted that the Maroons "are naturally alarmed at the continuance of cold and snow and express apprehension that they cannot maintain themselves by their labour in a cold country."
199. CO, vol. 69, p. 132, Letter, Chamberlain to Wentworth, 10 June 1798.
200. Ibid., Letter, Andrew Smith to Charles Samuels, 3 June 1797.
201. Governor's Letter Book, vol. 52, Letter, Wentworth to Portland, 2 June 1797. Dr. Oxley reported on 31 May 1797, "Our decrease in the whole is 19, allowing for the children born, and there is the greatest probability in a few weeks, that the excess will be 10 or 12, Thirty-two women being now big with child. I would ... recommend Inoculation in the end of the year, and previous thereto, during the summer months, frequent sea-bathing," CO, vol. 69, Letter, Oxley to Wentworth.
202. CO, vol. 68, Petition, James to Walpole, 23 April 1797.
203. CO, vol. 69, Petition of the Unfortunate Maroons, James to Walpole, 23 April 1797, and Ibid., Letter, Jarret to Portland, 12 August 1797.
204. Campbell, "Early Resistance," p. 97.
205. Raddall, p. 126.
206. *Columbian Centinel*, 16 December 1797, p. 1. Letter from "Humanitus" to B. Russell, Halifax, July 1797.
207. Campbell, *Back to Africa*, p. 16.
208. Ibid., pp. 23-4.

Chapter 7

209. Governor's Letter Book, vol. 51, #29, p. 357, Letter, Wentworth to Portland, 20 September 1796.
210. Ibid., pp. 347-8, Letter, Wentworth to Balcarres, 10 October 1796.
211. CO, vol. 67, Letter, Portland to Wentworth, 14 December 1796. On 16 December 1796 both Quarrell and Ochterlony were appointed justices of the Peace for the County of Halifax, Trider, *History of Dartmouth*, p. 363.
212. Campbell, *Nova Scotia*, p. 35.
213. Dallas, vol. 2, p. 479.
214. Akins, p. 112.
215. Dallas, vol. 2, p. 235. Flour had also been procured from the military stores, but it was not deemed acceptable. Even Prince Edward commented on the quality of the flour and butter sent to Nova Scotia, admitting the flour "was very bad." Letter Book of Prince Edward, Letter, #336, Prince Edward to Lord Commissioners of the Treasury, 1 June 1797. Both Quarrell and Ochterlony had become members of the Agricultural Society and promised to share the wheat, barley and rye seed that they received from England, "for the general interests of the province," Trider, *History of Dartmouth*, p. 364.
216. Governor's Letter Book, vol. 52, p. 10, Letter, Wentworth to Robert Liston, 17 February 1797.
217. Martin writes, "Colonel Quarrell had himself and his staff well provided with Dartmouth dwellings for he bought the three-story [*sic*] wooden house at north-

east corner of Portland and Commercial Streets," and "Colonel Quarrell also acquired the house formerly assigned Timothy Folger at the south east corner of Commercial and Queen Streets and a water-lot at the foot of that hill" (p. 105). Winks says, "Quarrell moved out in December" (p. 83).

218. Governor's Letter Book, vol. 51, p. 313, Letter, Wentworth to George Hammond, 16 August 1796, and Ibid., p. 357, # 2, Letter, Wentworth to Portland, 20 September 1796.

219. CO, vol. 69, Letter, Oxley to Wentworth, 16 June 1798.

220. Ibid., Letter, Howe to Wentworth, 8 June 1798.

221. Ibid., Letter, Gray to Wentworth, 18 June 1798.

222. *Columbian Centinel*, 16 December 1797, p. 1. Letter from "Humanitus" to B. Russell, Halifax, July 1797.

223. CO, vol. 69, pp. 125-31, Letter, Chamberlain to Wentworth, 10 June 1798.

224. Ibid.

225. CO, vol. 70, Letter, James Moody to Wentworth, 2 July 1799, paraphrased in Campbell, *Nova Scotia*, p. 132.

226. CO, vol. 69, Letter, Oxley to Wentworth, 2 July 1798.

227. Ibid., Letter, Howe to Wentworth, 8 June 1798.

228. CO, vol. 70, "Statement of Facts," in Campbell, *Nova Scotia*, p. 122.

229. CO, vol. 69, Letter, Chamberlain to Wentworth, 20 June 1798, paraphrased in Campbell, *Nova Scotia*, pp.75-7.

230. Winks points out that it was Ochterlony who had gone to Cuba to engage the infamous dogs and their handlers and that not all the Maroons trusted him (pp. 82-3). Campbell points out that Quarrell was commissioned by the government to procure the dogs. King George III, on receiving intelligence of this, expressed his "abhorrence of the mode of warfare" and ordered their removal, *Maroons*, pp. 229-230.

231. CO, vol. 69, Letter, Gray to Wentworth, 18 June 1798.

232. CO, vol. 68, Letter (with enclosures), Wentworth to Portland, 12 August 1797.

233. Conversely, this was a charge that was later levelled against Wentworth by Ochterlony in his examination before a committee of the Jamaican Legislative Assembly, Dallas, vol., 2, p. 491.

234. CO, vol. 69, p. 132, Letter, Chamberlain to Wentworth, 10 June 1798.

235. Ibid., p. 117, Letter, Gray to Wentworth, 18 June 1798.

236. Ibid., Letter, Chamberlain to Wentworth, 10 June 1798. A "seraglio" was the women's quarters in a Moslem house or palace, or, more pertinently here, a harem.

237. Ibid., Letter, Howe to Wentworth, 8 June 1798.

238. The product of Sir John's liaison was George Wentworth Colley, the progenitor of the family connection in Nova Scotia acknowledging its descent from the Lieutenant Governor. Lawson noted in 1893, "George Colley, an illegitimate coloured son of the great governor is still living ... He and his children and their children, as well, still own and live on the property," still known as the Governor's Farm. George W. Colley was not Wentworth's only illegitimate child. In 1798 Bridget Lowe gave birth to Edward H. Lowe, fathered by the governor. Raised in the home of Theophilus Chamberlain, Lowe became a prominent citizen of Dartmouth in business and as a churchman.

239. C0, vol. 68, Petition, James to Walpole, 23 April 1797.

240. Dallas suggests the initial chastisement of Ochterlony was prior to Quarrell's departure to New York on 23 February 1797, vol. 2, p. 234.

241. Wentworth says 20 May; Chamberlain says 24 May.

242. CO, vol. 69, p. 134, Letter, Chamberlain to Wentworth, 10 June 1798.

243. Governor's Letter Book, vol. 52, Letter, Wentworth to James and Smith.

244. Ibid., # 45, p. 67, Letter, Wentworth to Portland, 2 June 1797.

245. CO, vol. 69, p. 134, Letter, Chamberlain to Wentworth, 10 June 1798. Chamberlain says they "acceded promptly to the Condition, and appeared determined to go to work."

246. Ibid., Letter, Smith to Samuels, 3 July 1797. In this letter Smith stated to his brother, "the Governor has promised to write a good word to the king for our removal next year."

247. Governor's Letter Book, vol. 52, Letter, Wentworth to Portland, 10 July 1797.

248. Ibid.

249. Ibid., p. 95, Letter, Wentworth to Balcarres, 4 August 1797.

250. Ibid. Despite his dismissal, Ochterlony stayed in the Halifax area for a short time.

251. CO, vol. 70, "Statement of Facts. . .," in Campbell, *Nova Scotia*, pp. 124-5.

252. Winks, p. 84, n. 52.

253. CO, vol. 69, Letter, Wentworth to Portland, 12 August 1797.

254. Dunlop, vol.1, pp. 180, 187. Dunlop goes on, "[T]he Maroons are therefore now left to the brotherly love of Governor Wentworth and the commissioners are returning with petitions to the General Assembly for relief," (p. 185).

255. Dallas, vol. 2, p. 239.

256. Trider, *The History of the Dartmouth Quakers*, pp. 127-8. In June 1797 the Court of General Quarter Sessions of the Peace dealt with the request to build a new road "beginning in the old Street in the Dartmouth Shore near the boat house of Seth Coleman to run north to Preston. This would eventually be Ochterloney Street and join the new Preston Road" petitioned for in March 1797. Alexander Ochterlony had been one of the petitioners for this new road.

257. CO, vol. 69, Letter, Wentworth to Balcarres, 27 March 1798.

258. Kernaghan, pp. 429-30; Fergusson, *A Directory*, pp. 163-4; Calneck, pp. 212-5, 354-9; and Cuthbertson, *Johnny Bluenose*, pp. 133-7. Alexander Howe was Superintendent of the Maroons from July 1797 to July 1798. In 1802 he moved to a position as commissionary and store keeper (secured for him by Prince Edward) in the administration of Prince Edward Island. He was later a member of the Island's Council and justice of the peace. He returned to Nova Scotia in 1811 and died in Dartmouth in January 1813.

259. Letter Book of Prince Edward, Letter, #420, Prince Edward to Wentworth, 11 April 1797.

260. Governor's Letter Book, vol. 52, Letter, Wentworth to Portland, 12 August 1797.

261. CO, vol. 69, Letter, Chamberlain to Wentworth, 10 June 1798.

262. See Edwards, "Observations," p. 241.

263. C0, vol. 70, Letter, Wentworth to Portland, 30 May 1799.

264. CO, vol. 69, Letter, Gray to Wentworth, Preston, 18 June 1798.

265. *Journals*, Wednesday 28 June 1797, p. 251.

266. "Governor's answer," n. 19. The Speaker of the House and several other members of the Assembly went to Preston to determine for themselves whether the Maroons were likely to become successful settlers in Nova Scotia. In a 1799 deposition, Speaker Barclay affirmed support for Wentworth's decisions.

267. Governor's Letter Book, vol. 52, p. 149, Letter, Wentworth to Balcarres, 27 March 1798.

268. Ibid., #49, p. 84, Letter, Wentworth to Portland, 10 July 1797.

269. Ibid., Letter, Wentworth to Portland, 4 November 1797. See also Dallas, vol. 2, pp. 242-4.

270. Campbell, *Nova Scotia*, pp. 35-6.
271. Dallas, vol. 2, pp. 479, 493.
272. Governor's Letter Book, vol. 52, p. 159, Letter, Wentworth to Thomas McDonaugh, 28 April 1798. McDonaugh was a merchant in Boston.
273. Ibid., p. 9, n. 5, Letter, Wentworth to Balcarres, 4 August 1797.
274. Vol. 2, p. 244.
275. Governor's Letter Book, vol. 52, p. 95, Letter, Wentworth to Balcarres, 4 August 1797.
276. CO, vol. 68, Letter, Quarrell to Howe, 8 August 1797.
277. Ibid., Letter, Howe to Quarrell, 9 August 1797.
278. Cundall, p. 327.
279. Dallas, vol. 2, pp. 253-8. See also Campbell, *Nova Scotia*, pp. 53-4, where she points out that this address was not traced in either the Nova Scotia Archives or the Public Record Office, but from Dallas as noted. Campbell also noted, "According to Dallas, because of Quarrell's wish to leave the province as quickly as possible, fearing excess of emotions from the Maroons, they were not given the opportunity to present him the prepared address; it was finally sent to him in Boston en route to Jamaica."
280. Robinson, *The Iron Thorn*, p. 266.
281. Governor's Letter Book, vol. 52, p. 95, Letter, Wentworth to Balcarres, 4 August 1797.
282. Ibid., Letter, Portland to Wentworth, June 1797.
283. Dallas, vol. 2, pp. 244-9, n 57. In fact "5,580 was the exact amount, "ten pounds per head," voted to pay the bills of the Governor of Nova Scotia (p. 271).
284. *Columbian Centinel*, 16 December 1797, p. 1. Letter from "Humanitus" to B. Russell, Halifax, July 1797.
285. CO, vol. 69, Letter, Gray to Wentworth, 18 June 1798.
286. Governor's Letter Book, vol. 52, p. 179, n. 57, Letter, Wentworth to Portland, 23 June 1798.
287. CO, vol. 70, "Statement of Facts," in Campbell, *Nova Scotia*, p. 120.
288. Governor's Letter Book, vol. 52, p. 94, Letter, Wentworth to Tonge, 8 August 1797. For a discussion of the years-long enmity between Wentworth and Tonge, who has been called "Nova Scotia's first tribune of the people," see Ells and Tulloch. Cuthbertson provides an excellent analysis of Tonge and the Country Party, (*Johnny Bluenose*).
289. CO, vol. 69, Maroon Petition to His Majesty's Ministers, 12 August 1797.
290. Governor's Letter Book, vol. 52, p. 178, n.75, Letter, Wentworth to Portland, 23 June 1798.
291. CO, vol. 69, Letter, Howe to Wentworth, 8 June 1797.
292. Ibid., Letter, Chamberlain to Wentworth, 20 June 1797 [8].
293. Sutherland, p. 313.
294. Winks, p. 89. Perhaps the Maroons brought ". . .down from Preston to Bedford Basin" were housed at the Rockingham Barracks, one of the buildings located at Prince Edward's estate (formerly and again later owned by Wentworth), and located on the shores of Bedford Basin. See Tolson, p. 85. Also note the reference to the Music Rotunda and a possible connection to "Jamaican Voodoo." This suggestion is also found in Borrett, *Historic Halifax* p. 88. He states, "Legend has it that the Duke utilized the Maroons, coloured men who were shipped here from Jamaica, in his operations of building, and it is said that the rotunda was on occasions used as a kind of temple in which the Maroons practiced their rites."
295. CO, vol. 69, Letter, Gray to Wentworth, 18 June 1798.

296. CO, vol. 70, "Statement of Facts," in Campbell, *Nova Scotia*, p. 117-26.
297. Winks, p. 90, and CO, vol. 69, Letter, Portland to Wentworth, (Private) Whitehall, 8 March 1798. Quarrell stayed in the Halifax area until April 1798 when he sailed to Boston and finally arrived in Jamaica in October 1798. Quarrell denied writing any anonymous letters, but did admit to writing "letters under feigned names" (Humanitus?). See Dallas, vol. 2, p. 494. See also, CO, vol. 70, Maroon Petition to the House of Commons of Great Britain, n.d., as quoted in Campbell, *Nova Scotia*, pp. 91-2, where "beyond not thriving without the pineapple they also poetically stated that a West Indian could not be reconciled to Nova Scotia," and "that . . . Death in its most awful shapes" would be preferable "to a Residence in Nova Scotia."
298. Letter Book of Prince Edward, Letter, #356, Prince Edward to Wentworth, 15 July 1797, and Letter, Prince Edward to the Duke of York, 23 April 1797.
299. Winks, p. 85.
300. T.C. Haliburton, vol. 2, p. 259.
301. Governor's Letter Book, vol. 52, p. 146, Letter, Wentworth to Howe, 20 December 1797.
302. CO, vol. 69, Letter, Wentworth to Portland, (private), 10 March 1798.
303. Governor's Letter Book, v. 52, #54, p. 153, Letter, Wentworth to Portland, 24 April 1798.
304. See for example, Fergusson, *Diary*, p. 106. Simeon Perkins, a sitting MHA, noted in his diary on Wednesday, 4 July 1798, "We Adjourn Early, as Mr. Speaker [Thomas H. Barclay] and Some of the Leading Members are Invited to dine with Capt. Howe, at Preston, where he is stationed to take care of the Maroons."
305. T.C. Haliburton, vol. 2, p. 290.
306. Governor's Letter Book, vol. 52, p. 190, Letter, Wentworth to Howe, 9 July 1798. Martin states, "After some years in other services, Captain Howe returned to Dartmouth about 1811." He died there in 1813 and was likely buried in Christ Church Cemetery. His wife, Margaret Ann, the daughter of Benjamin Green, who had been the Provincial Treasurer of Nova Scotia, "died in her 75th year ... and was buried in Christ Church Cemetery ... probably alongside her husband" (p. 314).
307. Governor's Letter Book, vol. 52, p. 199, Letter, Wentworth to Chamberlain, 9 July 1798.
308. Tratt, p. 129.
309. Veilleux, p. 372. Hale became deputy paymaster general for Quebec in 1799.
310. Governor's Letter Book, vol. 52, #60, p. 235, Letter, Wentworth to Portland, 17 November 1798.

Chapter 8

311. Governor's Letter Book, vol. 52, p. 36, Letter, Wentworth to Clarence, 21 April 1797.
312. CO, vol. 69, p. 128, Letter, Chamberlain to Wentworth, 20 June 1798 (mistakenly dated 1797).
313. Campbell, *Back to Africa*, pp. 38, 45.
314. Governor's Letter Book, vol. 52, p. 95, Letter, Wentworth to Balcarres, 4 August 1797.
315. Ibid., #63, p. 278, Letter, Wentworth to Portland, 10 April 1799. See also Campbell, *Back to Africa*, pp. 22-3, 28, 57 and *passim*.
316. Campbell, *Back to Africa*, pp. 7, 27.

317. For example, "Before I set out this morning I saw Sam [Thorpe] give his brother a most wicked thrashing in the street — I made him desist. On enquiring, I found Tom had in the night got foul of a rather too young girl, which occasioned no small uproar being detected in the night," Campbell, *Back to Africa*, p. 26. Various similar incidents are related in Ross's Journal.

318. Raddall, p. 83.

319. Brown, pp. 127-8.

320. Raddall, p. 109.

321. Walker, "Royal Mistresses," p. 26.

322. CO, vol. 69, p. 115, Letter, John Moody to Wentworth, 12 June 1798.

323. Ibid., p. 103, Letter, Howe to Wentworth, 8 June 1798.

324. Campbell, *Back to Africa*, p. 36. There seems to have been a relationship between the station of the individual and the amount of rum supplied — i.e. Lawrence's wife 3 gallons, a baby 1/2 gallon (p. 37), a child 1 gallon, a captain 6 gallons (p. 30), Campbell's wife 1 gallon (p. 45), and so on. Rum was also used in both Nova Scotia and Sierra Leone as a reward. Ross noted that on the 21st November 1800 he "[g]ave Captain Parkinson a Gallon of Rum for having built the first house on his own lot" (p. 40).

325. Edwards noted, "[T]heir taste is so depraved that I have seen them drink new rum fresh from the still, in preference to wine which I offered them." See Edwards, "Observations," p. xxxix, and T.C. Haliburton, vol.2, pp. 294-5.

326. *Columbian Centinel*, 16 December 1797, p. 1. Letter from "Humanitus" to B. Russell, Halifax, July 1797.

327. Mavis Campbell notes, "[T]he Maroons never lost their implacable hatred for Balcarres, who betrayed them." In one of their numerous engaging petitions from Nova Scotia, they begged the King never to send "any of dem poor cotch Lord for Gubner again," *Maroons*, p. 257.

328. CO, vol. 69, Letter, Thomas Meanwell to Walpole, 23 April 1797, written at the request of Captain Smith.

329. See Dallas, vol. 2, pp. 481, 499, and Campbell, *Nova Scotia*, p. 53.

330. CO, vol. 69, Letter, Smith to Samuels, 3 June 1797.

331. Campell, *Maroons*, p. 227. See also Campbell, *Nova Scotia*, p. 255, n. 24, concerning Smith's wives.

332. CO, vol. 69, Letter, Smith to Samuels, 3 June 1797.

333. Carey Robinson observes, "[A]s is so often the case in protest groups there was a weak section that was inclined to give in to outside pressures. Some began to plant potatoes but the militants promptly beat them up," *Maroons*, p. 149. If Robinson is referring to the family and followers of James Palmer as "a weak section" then, based on Palmer's reputation, he is wrong.

334. C0, vol. 69, p. 100, Letter, Howe to Wentworth, 8 June 1798. Bilbo, usually spelled as the plural bilboas, was a long iron bar fastened at one end with a lock and with sliding shackles, used to confine prisoners' ankles.

335. Ibid., p. 108, Letter, Oxley to Wentworth, 16 June 1798. See also CO, vol. 68, Letter, Howe to Quarrell, 9 August 1797. Here Howe explains that those Maroons who planted potatoes at "Cold [*sic*] Harbour" had "made themselves obnoxious to some of the leading people among the Maroons and that they have been discouraged and severely treated by Mr. Ochterlony."

336. CO, vol. 68, Letter, Howe to Quarrell, 9 August 1797.

337. Winks, p. 81.

338. Governor's Letter Book, vol. 52, #49, p. 84, Wentworth to Portland, 10 July 1798.

339. Dallas, vol. 2, p. 240.

340. Dunlap, p. 185. See also Campbell, *Maroons*, pp. 233, 227-8.
341. Cundall, p. 330.
342. Registry of Deeds.
343. Winks, p. 90.
344. CO, vol. 69, Letter, Wentworth to Portland, 23 June 1798.
345. Ibid., Letter, Wentworth to Portland, 10 April 1799.
346. Ibid., Letter, Wentworth to Portland, 27 June 1799.
347. Ibid., Letter, Wentworth to Portland, 2 July 1799.
348. Ibid., Letter, Wentworth to Portland, 22 July 1799.
349. CO, vol. 70, Petition from the Boydville Maroons, 5 May 1799, quoted in Campbell, *Nova Scotia*, pp. 111-2.
350. Winks, p. 92.
351. CO, vol. 69, Letter, Wentworth to Portland, 16 August 1799.

Chapter 9

352. Cuthbertson, *The Loyalist Governor*, p. 16.
353. Ibid., p. 26.
354. Raddall, pp. 125, 137.
355. Cuthbertson, *The Loyalist Governor*, p. 53.
356. Ibid., p. 144.
357. Ibid., p. 93.
358. Winks, p. 86.
359. CO, vol. 69, Letter, Portland to Wentworth, June 1797.
360. Cuthbertson, *The Loyalist Governor*, p. 144.
361. Halifax merchant Lawrence Hartshorne, who profited from the Maroon settlement scheme, was a friend of Wentworth and the governor certainly favoured his firm for government business: "Between 1792 and 1795 Wentworth waxed very enthusiastic about the new flour mill which he had encouraged Hartshorne and Tremaine to build, and suggested that the army contract for flour be placed with them." Ells, p. 51.
362. Winks, p. 86.
363. Campbell, *Nova Scotia*, p. 261. Campbell includes the text of *Debrett's Parliamentary Debates*, pp. 262-77.
364. Winks, p. 87.
365. Cundall, p. 330. See also, CO, vol. 69, Letter, Walpole to Balcarres, 24 December 1795 (extract), and Winks, p. 88. Winks also points out that it was Walpole who had first thought of using the Cuban dogs in Jamaica — information of which the government was not yet aware.
366. Winks, pp. 86-8.
367. Ibid., p. 90.
368. Dallas, vol. 2, p. 282.
369. CO, vol. 69, Letter, Smith to Samuels, 3 June 1797. See also Dunlap, p. 186.
370. Ibid., Letter, Walpole to Portland, n.d, n.a., paraphrased in Campbell, *Nova Scotia*, p. 64.
371. Dallas, vol. 2, pp. 498-9.
372. Campbell, *Nova Scotia*, p. 53.
373. Dallas, vol. 2, p. 499.
374. Campbell, *Nova Scotia*, p. 123.
375. Dallas, vol. 2, p. 499.
376. CO, vol. 69, Letter, Smith to Samuels, 3 June 1797, printed in Campbell, *Nova*

Scotia, pp. 58-60.

377. Ibid., Letter (with enclosures), Walpole to Portland, July 1797, paraphrased in Campbell, *Nova Scotia*, p. 56.

378. Ibid., Letter, Portland to Walpole, 26 March 1798, reported in Campbell, *Nova Scotia*, p. 65.

379. Ibid., Letter, Walpole to Portland, 6 April 1798, paraphrased in Campbell, *Nova Scotia*, p 66.

380. CO, vol. 70, Letter and Statement of Facts, Wentworth to Portland, 30 May 1799. In Campbell, *Nova Scotia*, p. 12.

Chapter 10

381. Dallas, vol. 2, p. 282.

382. Winks, p. 90.

383. CO, vol. 70, Letter, Portland to the Chairman [Henry Thornton] of the Court of Directors of the Sierra Leone Company, 5 March 1799, quoted in Campbell, *Nova Scotia*, pp. 95-7.

384. Ibid., Dispatch, Unsigned to Governor and Council, Sierra Leone, 22 March 1799, quoted in Campell, *Nova Scotia*, pp. 100-5.

385. Ibid., Letter, Wentworth to Portland, 30 May 1799, quoted in Campbell, *Nova Scotia*, pp. 113-7.

386. Governor's Letter Book, vol. 52, #63, Letter, Wentworth to Portland, 13 April 1799. The order was not universally applied as Wentworth reported, "The aged, sick, young children — and women lying in. . .and schoolboys are allowed subsistence," #69, Letter, Wentworth to Portland, 22 July 1799. Murdoch states that fifty men of the Royal Nova Scotia Regiment under Captain Solomon were involved, vol. III, p. 177.

387. In November 1797 Prince Edward had recommended Captain Soloman for promotion, Letter Book of Prince Edward, Duke of Kent, Letter #404, Prince Edward to William Woodham, 19 November, 1797. The record is somewhat confusing about the stationing of soldiers at Preston. The document quoted above, and as supported in Campbell, *Nova Scotia*, pp. 107-8, points to 1799 as the year in question. Lawson, p. 175, Martin, p. 109, and Picart, p. 45, maintain it was in April 1797 that soldiers of the Royal Nova Scotia Regiment arrived in the heart of the Maroon settlement. Of course, it is possible and probable that troops were called upon twice.

388. Governor's Letter Book, vol. 52, #65, p. 295, Letter, Wentworth to Portland.

389. Ibid., #67, Letter, Wentworth to Portland, 27 June 1799.

390. Winks, pp. 91-2. See CO, vol. 70, Letter, Portland to Wentworth, 10 June 1799 (Secret), quoted in Campbell, *Nova Scotia*, pp. 130-1; CO, vol. 70, Letter, Portland to Wentworth, 9 October 1799, in which Portland makes it clear that the Maroons are not to be consulted on the matter and reiterates that Wentworth is to ensure that "every one of the Maroons is embarked without any exception being made on any account."

391. CO, vol. 70, Letter, Wentworth to Portland, 5 May 1799, quoted in Campbell, *Nova Scotia*, p. 110.

392. Winks, p. 92.

393. Ibid., p. 85.

394. Dallas, vol. 2, pp. 477-505. See also, CO, vol. 70, "Statement of Facts. . .," quoted in Campbell, *Nova Scotia*, pp. 117-26.

395. Governor's Letter Book, vol. 52, #67, p. 305, Letter, Wentworth to Portland, 2

July 1799.

396. See Governor's Letter Book, vol. 52, #78, p. 365, Letter, Wentworth to Portland, 21 December 1799. Perhaps Wentworth was not completely forthcoming. The Nova Scotia Provincial Museum Report (1934-1935) states that in 1804, he had a "child by a beautiful Maroon woman. He kept her in Nova Scotia after all the other Maroons were sent off to Africa in 1800." This woman was most likely Sarah Colley.

397. CO, vol. 70, Letter, Wentworth to John King, 18 August 1799. King was Under-Secretary of State.

398. Governor's Letter Book, vol. 53, p. 11, Letter, Wentworth to King, 23 February 1800.

399. CO, vol. 70, Letter, Wentworth to Portland, 22 October 1799.

400. Governor's Letter Book, vol. 53, p. 11, Letter, Wentworth to King, 23 February 1800.

401. Governor's Letter Book, vol. 52, #77, Letter, Wentworth to Portland, 22 October 1799. Winks states that the *Asia* did not leave Britain until the second week of October but obviously there is some confusion over dates (p. 92).

402. Governor's Letter Book, vol. 52, #78, Letter, Wentworth to Portland, 21 December 1799.

403. Winks, p. 92.

404. MG 15, v. 10, n. 35. According to Wentworth's complaints, Moody went to Jamaica, enticed by Quarrell to leave Nova Scotia and who found him employment there. CO, vol. 70, "Statement of Facts. . . ," quoted in Campbell, *Nova Scotia*, p. 126 and *passim.*

405. MG 15, vol. 10, n. 6.

406. Ibid. Dr. Michael Head was born in Ireland and began to practice medicine in Nova Scotia about 1765. In 1777 he was appointed a surgeon at the General Hospital in Halifax. "By 1790 he was operating a drug and apothecary shop on Hollis Street, a business he continued, along with the practice of surgery, until he died on June 11, 1808." See Marble, pp. 74-5. Oxley resigned his position due to a reduction in his income and took passage to England as early as 17 November 1798. See CO, vol. 69, p. 220, Letter, Wentworth to Portland, 17 November 1798. He was replaced by Dr. John Fraser (b. Islay 1754-d. Windsor, N.S., 1818), who had come to North America as a surgeon attached to the King's Orange Rangers and saw service in the American Revolutionary War. When the regiment was reduced he received land grants in Nova Scotia and settled there to improve his land and work as a surgeon in Windsor. He was surgeon to the Royal Nova Scotia Regiment and, on Oxley's departure, was appointed Surgeon to the Maroons. Marble points out that Fraser had regular connections with militia units and after the RNS Regiment was reduced he became surgeon to the Nova Scotia Fencibles. In a regular report on the health of the Maroons, Fraser commented on 31 May 1799 that they were generally in good health and that the discontinuation of their food allowance had not created any real problems in that no one had died for want of food. They still had fish from their "winter stores," money saved, and a supply of poultry. He completely discounted the "odious" reports that had spread attributing several deaths to the suspension of their food allowance. Fraser also commented on the affection of the Maroons for their children, that the school was doing well, and lamented that they would not work as hard for themselves as they would for others. See CO, vol. 70, Report, Fraser to Wentworth.

407. Governor's Letter Book, vol. 52, #78, Letter, Wentworth to Portland, 21

December 1799.

408. Ibid., #81, *Letter*, Wentworth to Portland, 10 June 1800.

409. Winks, p. 93.

410. Campbell, *Back to Africa*, p. xx; Walker, *Black Loyalists*, p. 242; and Winks, pp. 93-4.

411. Governor's Letter Book, vol. 53, p. 2, Letter, Wentworth to King, 20 January 1800. Winks reports that Ross was Captain of the *Asia*, but this was not the case (p. 93).

412. Governor's Letter Book, vol. 52, #78, Letter, Wentworth to Portland, 21 December 1799.

413. Ibid., #77, Letter, Wentworth to Portland, 22 October 1799.

414. CO, vol. 74, Letter, Wentworth to John Gray, acting Governor, and Thomas Ludlam, 2nd in Council, Sierra Leone, 5 August 1800, quoted in Campbell, *Nova Scotia*, pp. 159-61. Gray had earlier cautioned Wentworth to "be particularly careful and backward making promises to the Maroons in regard to what is likely to be their situation here." See Campbell, *Nova Scotia*, pp. 144-9.

415. Governor's Letter Book, v. 52, #77, Letter, Wentworth to Portland, 22 October 1799.

416. Ibid., #63, p. 278, Letter, Wentworth to Portland, [10?] April 1799.

417. Ibid., vol. 53, p. 124, Letter, Wentworth to John Gray, 5 August 1800.

418. Ibid., #81, Letter, Wentworth to Portland, 10 June 1800.

419. Martell, p. 13.

420. Borrett, "The Maroons," p. 33.

421. Governor's Letter Book, vol. 53, p. 160, Letter, Wentworth to the Commissioners of Transports, 6 November 1800.

422. This was not the first time the *Asia* had visited the port. It was in Halifax in November 1796 "with Governor Campbell and his family being unable to land in Bermuda due to a gale," *Royal Gazette*, 8 November 1796.

423. Governor's Letter Book, vol. 53, #81, p. 88, Letter, Wentworth to Portland, 10 June 1800.

424. Ibid., p. 88, Letter, Wentworth to Sheriff, 6 June 1800, and p. 92, Letter, Wentworth to Sheriff, 18 June 1800.

425. Ibid., p. 124, Letter, Wentworth to Gray, 5 August 1800.

Chapter 11

426. Ibid., #83, p. 122, Letter, Wentworth to Portland, 28 July 1800.

427. Ibid., p. 166, Letter, Wentworth to Commissioner of Transports, 6 November 1800.

428. Ibid., p. 122, Letter, Wentworth to Portland, 28 July 1800.

429. Ibid., p. 124, Letter, Wentworth to Gray, 5 August 1800.

430. Ibid., #64, p. 129, Letter, Wentworth to Portland, 6 August 1800.

431. Winks writes, "except those who are ill," rather than giving the specific number, but the document is clear (p. 93).

432. Campbell, *Back to Africa*, p. 23.

433. Governor's Letter Book, vol. 53, p. 124, Letter, Wentworth to Gray, 5 August 1800. Wilson writes that the terms included a clause stating that the Maroons were not to be allowed guns. Their land grants were on much the same basis as the Loyalists, except the quit rent was stipulated and conditions regarding cultivation were attached.

434. Indeed, other sources claim that as many as eighteen Maroons "ran and hid in

what we call the Preston Barrens to avoid being deported to Sierra Leone," Bruce Johnson as quoted in Dorey. Campbell, *Nova Scotia*, p. xvi, discusses her perceptions about local attitudes towards the Maroons and the historical record. She states that during her "first field trip in 1976, I found that almost every Afro-Canadian I interviewed claimed Maroon heritage. These were mainly from the Dartmouth and Preston areas. However, upon my second and third visits in 1982 and 1987 respectively, I found no such claim to Maroon ancestry." Campbell postulates that younger people had "discovered a new Canadian nationalism ... stressing civil rights for blacks" and "black contribution to Canadian society." She concludes by stating, "Their earlier claim to Maroon heritage had more to do with a search for a positive image or symbol to promote a favourable identity than with historical/genealogical reality. For, as far as we know, all the Maroons did leave Nova Scotia for Sierra Leone, with some doubt concerning only four of them." Winks, p. 92, n. 67, states "that Maroons remained at Tracadie and Preston respectively; but the first is definitely mistaken and the second probably so." His sources are Antigonish *Casket*, 8 July 1943; and Brown, *Place Names*, p. 19.

435. pp. 93-4. See also Campbell, *Nova Scotia*, pp. 163-249.
436. Governor's Letter Book, vol. 53, #84, p. 129, Letter, Wentworth to Portland, 6 August 1800. Winks writes that they departed on 3 August but that is incorrect (p. 93).
437. Silver claims, "Great was the rejoicing in Halifax as the "Asia" sailed away with her freight of black freebooters" (p. 189). However, he provides no evidence and his opinion may be more the expression of 1900 than 1800. Picart writes that their departure was "resented" (p. 51).
438. Governor's Letter Book, vol. 52, #67, p. 305, Letter, Wentworth to Portland, 2 July 1799.
439. Ibid., #65, p. 295, Letter, Wentworth to Portland, 30 May 1799.
440. Ibid., vol. 53, p. 124, Letter, Wentworth to Gray, 5 August 1800.
441. Ibid., vol. 52, #65, p. 295, Letter, Wentworth to Portland, 30 May 1799.
442. Ibid., p. 377, Letter, Wentworth to R. Molesworth, 15 January 1800.
443. Ibid., vol. 53, p. 124, Letter, Wentworth to Gray, 5 August 1800.
444. Ibid.
445. Winks, p. 95.
446. Ibid.
447. Governor's Letter Book, vol. 52, p. 377, Letter, Wentworth to R. Moleworth [sic], 15 January 1800.
448. Ibid., vol. 53, p. 124, Letter, Wentworth to Gray, 5 August 1800.z
449. Winks, p. 94.
450. Governor's Letter Book, vol. 53, #83, p. 122, Letter, Wentworth to Portland, 23 July 1800.
451. Campbell, *Back to Africa*, p. 1.
452. While George Ross does not completely disappear from the records following the end of his journal, his role with the Maroons was limited by his other responsibilities with the Company, and his personal interests in independent trade.
453. For which the Maroons, according to Campbell, "gave many hundred brandy tanks," *Back to Africa*, p. 4. The extent to which Captain John Sheriff was a part of the fraud is judged by Campbell to be "somewhat," "either from poor supervision or from collusion with his steward, Jarrett" (p. 1). Winks states that the steward was a black loyalist (p. 94), but Campbell identifies him as "Old John

Jarrett, a Maroon." See also Campbell, *Nova Scotia*, p. 58.

454. Campbell, *Back to Africa*, pp. 2, 24 and n. 48. Lieutenant L. Smith, involved in the suppression of the Nova Scotian rebellion in Sierra Leone, "was promoted on the strength of this action and began a distinguished career which included governorships in Barbados and Jamaica. His mother was the novelist Charlotte Smith." See Wilson, p. 403, n.37.

455. Campbell, *Back to Africa*, p. 23. Sierra Leone, situated on the Atlantic Ocean in West Africa is about one quarter larger than Nova Scotia (71,740 km^2 to 55,491 km^2). Its population in 2000 was over seven times larger. Its capital, then and now, is Freetown, which was founded in 1787 as a settlement for freed slaves. Guinea on the north and east, and Liberia on the south, are its neighbours. The Portuguese were the first European explorers and they gave Sierra Leone ("lion mountains") its name. In 1808 its Charter was altered and Sierra Leone became a British, as opposed to a company, colony. It became independent in 1961 and a republic in 1971. Its recent history (not unlike the events that marked the arrival of the Maroons) has been troubled by military dictatorship and civil war.

456. Campbell, "Early Resistance," pp. 102-3; *Back to Africa*, pp. xvi-xvii.

457. Walker, *Black Loyalists*, p. 233.

458. Ibid., p. 234. See also Crooks, p. 56.

459. Robinson, *Fighting*, p. 152.

460. Within Freetown, "Nova Scotians lived at first separately from Maroons in their own section," Fyle, p. 39.

461. A somewhat controversial place at times. See Walker, *Black Loyalists*, pp. 241-3, and Fife, for examples.

462. Dallas, vol. 2, p. 288. Robinson writes, "It is doubtful if any of the adult generation of Trelawnys who participated in the conflict of 1795 ever returned to Jamaica; but it is known that towards the middle of the nineteenth century Trelawnys did return, perhaps the children or grand children of the exiles," *The Iron Thorn*, p. 270.

Chapter 12

463. Governor's Letter Book, vol. 52, p. 324, Letter, Wentworth to Balcarres, 24 September 1799.

464. Ibid., vol. 53, p. 485, Letter, Wentworth to Bremmer, 11 March 1804.

465. Some of the property was sold in 1799. C.B. Fergusson, F.3, contains a record of sale of several relatively small lots to Theophilus Chamberlain.

466. Governor's Letter Book, vol. 53, p. 2, Letter, Wentworth to King, 20 January 1800.

467. Ibid., #81, p. 88, Letter, Wentworth to Portland, 10 June 1800.

468. "Governor's answer," n. 127.

469. Trider, *The History of the Dartmouth Quakers*, p. 133.

470. MG 15, v. 10, #1 to #64.

471. Governor's Letter Book, vol. 53, p. 207, Letter, Wentworth to B. Cable, 25 April 1801.

472. Fingard, p. 851.

473. Governor's Letter Book, vol. 53, p. 514, Letter, Wentworth to the Lords Commissioners of the Treasury, 23 June 1804. In 1804 Chamberlain received £111.2.21/2 for his work between 1 February 1801 and 8 May 1804, which largely consisted of "adjusting, arranging, and making out all the Maroon Accounts since 30 June 1800 to the final close of them, making Duplicates and Triplicates

of the same and making a final settlement of the concern," MG 15, v. 10, n. 63.

474. Fingard, p. 851.

475. Cuthbertson, *The Loyalist Governor*, p. 146. Sir Charles Mary Wentworth was the only child of Sir John and Lady Wentworth. Named for his godparents, the Marquis and Marchioness of Rockingham, he graduated from Oxford and acted as private secretary to Earl Fitzwilliam when the latter was Lord of the Treasury, and was a member of the Council of Nova Scotia. He succeeded to the baronetcy on his father's death. He died unmarried at Kingsland, Devon, 10 April 1844, whereupon the baronetcy became extinct. He left Prince's Lodge and other lands, and Sir John's papers, to his cousin, the author Mrs. Catherine Gore.

476. T.C. Haliburton, vol. 2, p. 291.

477. Winks, p. 91, n. 65.

478. Cuthbertson states, "That in the early 1800s Wentworth was able to stay out of debtors" prison was due solely to his being governor," *The Loyalist Governor*, p. 94.

Conclusion

479. Martin, p. 273, n. 1.

480. See CO, vol. 70, Petition from Benjamin Gray (a Maroon) to Wentworth, n.d., in Campbell, *Nova Scotia*, p. 112.

481. See CO, vol. 74, Document 118, "An Account of Maroon Property Embarked with them from Nova Scotia to Sierra Leone."

BIBLIOGRAPHY

Primary Sources: Archival

A Catalogue of Dispatches from the Secretary of State to the Governors of Nova Scotia from 1800 to 1806 and from 1806 to 1832; collected and arranged under direction of Thomas B. Aikins, Commissioner of Public Records at Halifax, N.S., 1860. RG 1, vol. 70. Nova Scotia Archives and Records Management (NSARM).

C.B. Fergusson fonds. MG 1, vol. 1844. NSARM.

Colonial Office Records, Nova Scotia. CO 217, vols, 67-70. National Archives of Canada/Great Britain Public Record Office. mfm. NSARM

Daniel Cobb Harvey fonds. NSARM.

Executive Council Minutes, 28 January 1799-30 August 1809. RG 1, vol. 191. NSARM.

"Governor's answer to Resolutions respecting the Maroons, 29 June 1797." RG 1, vol. 419. NSARM.

Governor's Letter Book. RG 1, vols. 51, 52, 53, 54. NSARM.

Head Quarters Office, #3, District and Garrison Orders. MG 12. NSARM.

Head Quarters Office, Record of Corps and Regiments which have served in the Nova Scotia command since 1783. MG 12. mfm 9216. NSARM.

Letter Book of Prince Edward, the Duke of Kent, from September 1794 to May 1800. ADD. 7/57-698. Royal Archives (Windsor Castle).

MG 15, vol. 10, #1-64. NSARM.

MG 100, vol. 214, #17-171. NSARM.

Militia Records of Nova Scotia, 1 June 1778 – 14 March 1866. RG 1, vols. 440-442. NSARM.

National Archives of Canada, British Military and Naval Records, Series "C." MG 12. NSARM.

Phyllis R. Blakeley fonds. MG 1, vol. 3025. NSARM.

Registry of Deeds, Halifax County, N.S. Books 21, 22, 32.

RG 22, No. 1 Staff Office records 1781 – 1833, No. 10 Halifax County 1791-1830, No. 21 Officer's Accounts 1794-1796, No. 22 Officer's Accounts 1797-1802, No. 23 Adjutant General: Correspondence 1749-1813, No. 36 #5 Commissions-Militia 1749-1917. NSARM.

Thomas, C. E. Calendar to the Microfilm Collection of the Society for the Propagation of the Gospel in Foreign Parts, n.d. Typescript, NSARM.

War Office in Letters, Nova Scotia. MG 12, vol. 18, 1795-1800. NSARM.

Primary Sources: Printed

Journals and Proceedings of the House of Assembly, 1796-1808. Halifax: King's Printer, 1791-1809.

Wentworth, Sir John. *Extracts and copies of letters from Sir John, Wentworth, lieutenant governor of Nova Scotia to His Grace the Duke of Portland respecting the settlement of the Maroons in that province,* 10 April 1797.

_____. *Papers relative to the Settling of the Maroons in His Majesty's Province of Nova Scotia.* Ordered to be printed 22nd February 1798.

Newspapers — Halifax, N.S.:

Weekly Chronicle, 1796-1800

Halifax Journal, 1796-1800

Royal Gazette and Nova Scotia Advertiser, 1796-1800

Halifax Chronicle, 1942

Halifax Evening Mail, 1934

Mail Star, 1997

Newspapers — Boston, Mass.:

Columbian Centinel, 1797.

Secondary Sources

Archibald, Sir Adams."Life of Sir John Wentworth, Governor of Nova Scotia,"
    Collections of the Nova Scotia Historical Society, XX (1921), 43-109.
_____. "Story of Deportation of Negroes to Sierra Leone." *Collections of the
    Nova Scotia Historical Society*, VII (1891), 129-54.
Ajayi, J.F. Ade and J.D.Y. Peel, eds. *People and Empires in African History: Essays in
    Memory of Michael Crowder.* New York: Longman, 1992.
Akins, Thomas Beamish. "History of Halifax City," *Collections of the Nova Scotia
    Historical Society*, VIII (1895), 3-272.
Augier, F.R., S.C. Gordon, D.G. Hall, M. Reckord. *The Making of the West Indies.*
    London: Longman, 1972.
Bertley, L.W. *Canada and Its People of African Descent.* Pierrefonds, PQ: Bilongo,
    1977.
Bilby, Kenneth M. "How the 'Older Heads' Talk: A Jamaican Maroon Spirit Possession
    Language and its Relationship to the Creoles of Suriname and Sierra Leone,"
    Nieuwe West-Indische Gids/New West Indian Guide. 57 (1/2) 1983, pp. 37-88.
_____. *Partisan Spirits: Ritual Interaction and Maroon Identity in Eastern
    Jamaica.* M.A. thesis, Wesleyan University, 1979.
_____. "The Kromanti Dance of the Windward Maroons of Jamaica," *Nieuwe
    West-Indische Gids/New West Indian Guide.* 55 (1/2) 1981, pp. 52—101.
Binns, Margaret and Tony Binns. *Sierra Leone.* The World Bibliographical Series, vol.
    148. Oxford, G.B.: Clio Press, 1992.
Black, Cliton V. *The Story of Jamaica.* London: Collins, 1965.
Borrett, William Coates. *East Coast Port and Other Tales Told Under the Old Town
    Clock.* Halifax, N.S. Imperial, 1944.
_____. *Down East: Another Cargo of Tales Told Under the Old Town Clock.*
    Halifax: Imperial, 1945.
_____. *Historic Halifax in Tales Told Under the Old Town Clock.* Toronto:
    Ryerson, 1948.
Boyd, Frank, ed. *McKerrow: A Brief History of Blacks in Nova Scotia (1783 —1895).*
    Halifax: Afro-Nova Scotian Enterprises, 1976.
Bridges, George Wilson. *The Annals of Jamaica.* 2 vols. London: Frank Cass, (1828)
    1968.
Brown, Thomas J. *Place-Names of the Province of Nova Scotia.* n.l.: n.p., 1922.
Brown, Wallace. "Byles, Mather." In Halpenny, vol. V, 1801-1820, pp. 127-8.
Brymner, Douglas. "The Jamaica Maroons — How they came to Nova Scotia — How
    they left it," *Transactions of the Royal Society of Canada*, Second Series, I (1895),
    pp. 81-90.
Calnek, W.A. *History of the County of Annapolis.* (Edited and completed by
    A.W.Savary). Toronto: Briggs, 1897/Belleville, Ont.: Mika, 1972.
Campbell, Duncan. *Nova Scotia in its Historical, Mercantile and Industrial Relations.*
    Montreal: Lovell, 1873.
Campbell, G.C. *The History of Nova Scotia.* Toronto: Ryerson, 1948.
Campbell, Mavis C. *Back to Africa, George Ross and the Maroons: From Nova Scotia to
    Sierra Leone.* Trenton, NJ: Africa World Press, 1993.
_____. "Early Resistance to Colonialism: Montague James and the Maroons in

Jamaica, Nova Scotia and Sierra Leone." In Ajayi, pp. 89—105.

_____. *The Maroons of Jamaica 1655-1796: A History of Resistance, Collaboration & Betrayal.* Trenton, N.J.: Africa World Press, 1990.

_____, ed. *Nova Scotia and the Fighting Maroons: A Documentary History.* Studies in Third World Societies. Publication #41. Williamsburg, Va: College of William and Mary, January 1990.

Craton, Michael. "Jamaican Slavery." In Engerman and Genovese, eds., pp. 249-84

Crooks, J.J. *A History of the Colony of Sierra Leone, Western Africa.* London: Frank Cass, 1903.

Cundall, Frank. *Historic Jamaica.* Kingston, Jamaica: Institute of Jamaica, 1915.

Cuthbertson, Brian C. *Johnny Bluenose at the Poles: Epic Nova Scotian Election Battles 1758—1848.* Halifax: Formac, 1994.

_____. *The Loyalist Governor: Biography of Sir John Wentworth.* Halifax, N.S.: Petheric Press, 1983.

Dallas, Robert Charles. *The History of the Maroons from their origin to the establishment of their chief tribe at Sierra Leone: including the expedition to Cuba, for the purpose of procuring Spanish chasseurs; and the State of the Island of Jamaica for the last ten years: with a Succinct History of the Island previous to that period.* 2 vols. London: Longman & Rees, 1803/London: Frank Cass, 1968.

Dorey, Barry. "Memorial to Maroons unveiled in Dartmouth," *Mail Star,* 8 September 1997, Section A4.

Dridzo, A.D. "The Origin of the Second Maroon War, 1795-1796. A Planter's Conspiracy?" *Jamaican Journal.* 6, 1 (March, 1977) pp. 21-5. This paper is an an extract from A.D. Dridzo. *Jamaican Maroons.* Trans. Alex Gradussor. Moscow: [Nauka/Navia?], 1971.

Durham, Katherine. *Journal to Accompong.* Walport, Connecticut: Negro University Press, (1946) 1971.

Dunlap, William. *Diary of William Dunlap (1766-1839).* 3 vols. *Collections of the New York Historical Society for the Year 1929.* 1930. New York/London: Blom, 1969.

Dunn, Richard S. *Sugar and Slaves: The Rise of the Planter Class in the English West Indies, 1624-1713.* Chapel Hill, NC: The University of North Carolina Press, 1972.

Earle, Stafford. *The Basic Jamaica Book.* Etobicoke, Ont.: ECI Publications, 1977.

Edwards, Bryan. "Observations on the Disposition, Character, Manner, and Habits of Life, of the Maroon Negroes of the Island of Jamaica; and a Detail of the Origin, Progress, and Termination of the late War between those People and the White Inhabitants." In Price, *Maroon Societies,* pp. 239-40.

_____. *The Proceedings of the Governor and Assembly of Jamaica, in Regard to the Maroons Negroes and a detail of the Late war between those People and the White Inhabitants.* London: John Stockade, 1796.

Edwards, Plimsoll J. "The Militia of Nova Scotia." *Collections of the Nova Scotia Historical Society,* XVII (1913), pp. 63-110.

Ells, Margaret. "Governor Wentworth's Patronage," *Collections of the Nova Scotia Historical Society,* XXV (1942), pp. 49-73.

Engerman, Stanley and Eugene D. Genovese, eds. *Race and Slavery in the Western Hemisphere: Quantitative Studies.* Princeton, NJ: Princeton University Press, 1975.

Fenerty, Mrs. Robert. "How Maroon Hill Got its Name and a Short History of the Folks Now There." Typescript, Public Archives of Nova Scotia, 1955.

Fergusson, Charles Bruce, ed. *The Diary of Simeon Perkins, 1797-1803.* Toronto: The Champlain Society, 1967.

_____, ed. *A Documentary Study of the Establishment of the Negroes in Nova Scotia between the War of 1812 and the Winning of Responsible Government.* Halifax: Publication No. 8, The Public Archives of Nova Scotia, 1948.

_____, ed. *A Directory of the Members of the Legislative Assembly of Nova Scotia, 1758-1958.* Halifax, N.S.: The Public Archives of Nova Scotia, 1958.

Fingard, Judith. "Wentworth, Sir John." In Halpenny, vol. V, 1801-1820, pp. 848-52.

Fyfe, Christopher A. *A History of Sierra Leone.* London: Oxford University Press, 1962.

Fyle, C. Magbaily. *The History of Sierra Leone: A Concise Introduction.* New York: Evan Brothers, 1981.

Gardner, W.J. *A History of Jamaica.* (1st edition 1873) London: Frank Cass, 1971.

Genovese, Eugene D. *From Rebellion to Revolution: Afro-American Slave Revolts in the Making of the New World.* Baton Rouge: Louisiana State University Press, 1979.

Gillen, Mollie. *The Prince and His Lady: The Love Story of the Duke of Kent and Madame de St. Laurent.* Toronto: Griffin House, 1970.

Grant, John N. "Black Immigration into Nova Scotia, 1776-1815." *Journal of Negro History.* LVIII, 3 (1973), pp. 253-70.

_____. *Black Nova Scotians.* Halifax: Nova Scotia Museum, 1980.

_____. *The Immigration and Settlement of the Black Refugees of the War 1812 in Nova Scotia and New Brunswick.* Cherrybrook: The Black Cultural Centre for Nova Scotia, 1990.

_____. "The Origins of Maroon Hill." *Sackville Heritage Society Newsletter.* 1, 2 (December, 1980), pp. 9-20.

Haliburton, George. "The Nova Scotia Settlers of 1792." *Sierra Leone Studies,* New Series, III (1954), pp. 16-25.

Haliburton, Thomas Chandler. *An Historical and Statistical Account of Nova Scotia.* 2 vol. Halifax: Joseph Howe, 1829.

Halpenny, F.G. and J. Hamelin, eds. *Dictionary of Canadian Biography.* Toronto/Montréal: University of Toronto Press/Les presses de l'université Laval, 1983, 1987.

Hamilton James C. "The Africans in Canada: The Maroons of Jamaica and Nova Scotia." Extract from *Proceedings of the Canadian Institute,* 1890, pp. 1-10.

Hamilton, James C. "The Maroons of Jamaica and Nova Scotia," *Proceedings of the Canadian Institute.* Third Series, VII (1888- 1889), pp. 260-9.

Harris, Reginald V. *The Church of St. Paul in Halifax, Nova Scotia: 1749-1949.* Toronto: Ryerson, 1949.

Higman, B.W. *Slave Populations of the British Caribbean, 1807-1834.* Baltimore: Johns Hopkins University Press, 1984.

Hill, Daniel G. *The Freedom Seekers: Blacks in Early Canada.* Argencourt, Ont.: Book Society of Canada, 1981.

Hurwitz, Samuel J. and Edith F Hurwitz. *Jamaica: A Historical Portrait.* New York: Praeger, 1941.

James, C.L.R. *The Black Jacobins: Toussaint L'Ouverture and the San Domingo Revolution.* 2nd ed. New York: Vintage, 1963.

Kernaghan, Lois K. "Howe, Alexander." In Halpenny, vol. V. 1801-1820, pp. 429-30.

Lawson, Mary Jane Katzmann. *History of the Townships of Dartmouth, Preston and Lawrencetown, Halifax County, N.S.* Akins Historical Prize Essay, (ed. Harry Piers) Halifax: Morton, 1893/Belleville, Ont.: Mika, 1972.

Lee, Sidney, ed. *Dictionary of National Biography.* vol. 33/59, London: Smith, Elder, 1893/1899.

Long, Edward. *The History of Jamaica.* 3 vols. London: Frank Cass, (1774) 1970.

MacKerrow, Richard. *A Brief History of the Colored Baptists of Nova Scotia.* Halifax:

Nova Scotia Printing Company, 1895.

MacLeod, Andrew, ed. *St. John's Anglican Church Westphal: Founded 1791.* Darthmouth: St. John's Anglican Church Bicentennial Society, 1989.

MacNutt, W.S. *The Atlantic Provinces: The Emergence of Colonial Society, 1712-1857.* Toronto: McClelland and Stewart, 1965.

_____. "Edward Augustus." In Halpenny, vol. V, 1801-1820, pp. 296-8.

Marble, Alan E., "A History of Medicine in Nova Scotia, 1784-1854." *Collections of the Royal Nova Scotia Historical Society*, 41 (1982), pp. 73-101.

Martell, James Stuart. *The Romance of Government House.* rev. ed. Halifax: Nova Scotia Government Services, 1973.

Martin, J. P. *History of Dartmouth, N.S.* Halifax: Atlantic Nova Print, 1957.

McFarlane, Milton. *Cudjoe the Maroon.* London: Allison and Biesley, 1977.

Morrison, James H. *Wave to Whisper: British Military Communication in Halifax and the Empire, 1780-1880.* History and Archeology, No. 64, Parks Canada, 1982.

Murdoch, Beamish. *A History of Nova Scotia or Acadia.* 3 vols. Halifax: James Barnes, 1865-1867.

Nelson, R.R. *The Home Office, 1782-1801.* Durham, NC: Duke University Press, 1969.

Pacey, Elizabeth. *Halifax Citadel.* Halifax: Nimbus, 1985.

Pachai, Bridglal. *Beneath the Clouds of the Promised Land: The Survival of Nova Scotia's Blacks, vol. 1: 1600-1800.* Halifax: Black Educators' Association, 1987.

_____. *Beneath the Clouds of the Promised Land: The Survival of Nova Scotia's Blacks, vol. 2: 1800-1989.* Halifax: Black Educators' Association, 1990.

_____. *Peoples of the Maritimes: Blacks.* Tantallon, N.S.: Four East Publications, 1987.

Parry, J.H. and P. Sherlock. *A Short History of the West Indies.* 3rd ed., London: MacMillan, 1971.

Pascoe, C.F. *Two Hundred Years with the S.P.G.: An Historical Account of the Society for the Propagation of the Gospel in Foreign Parts, 1701-1900.* London: The Society for the Propagation of the Gospel, 1901.

Patterson, Orlando. "Slavery and Slave Revolts: A Sociohistorical Analysis of the First Maroon War, 1655-1740," in Price, ed., *Maroon Societies*, pp. 246-92.

Payzant, Joan M. and Louis J. Payzant. *Like a Weaver's Shuttle: A History of the Halifax- Darmouth Ferries.* Halifax: Nimbus, 1979.

Philalethes, Demoticus. "Hunting the Maroons with Dogs in Cuba." In Price, *Maroon Societies*, pp. 60-3.

Picart, Lennox O'Riley. "The Trelawny Maroons and Sir John Wentworth: The Struggle to Maintain their Cututure, 1796-1800." M.A. thesis, University of New Brunswick, 1993.

Picart, Lennox O'Riley. "The Trelawny Maroons and Sir John Wentworth: The Struggle to Maintain their Culture, 1796-1800." *Collections of the Royal Nova Scotia Historical Society*, 44 (1996) pp. 165-87.

Piers, Harry. *The Evolution of the Halifax Fortress, 1749-1928.* Publication #7. Halifax: Public Archives of Nova Scotia, 1947.

Pigou, Elizabeth. "A Note on Afro-Jamaican Beliefs and Rituals." *Jamaican Journal*, 20, 2 (May-June, 1987), pp. 23-6.

Price, Richard, ed. *The Guiana Maroons: A Historical and Bibliographical Introduction.* Baltimore: Johns Hopkins University Press, 1976.

_____, ed. *Maroon Societies: Rebel Slave Communities in the Americas.* 3rd ed. Baltimore: Johns Hopkins University Press, 1996.

Raddall, Thomas H. *Halifax: Warden of the North.* New York: Doubleday, 1965.

Report on the Provincial Museum and Science Library 1934-35. Halifax, N.S.: King's Printer, 1935.

Roberts, Theodore Goodridge. "Sir John's Mansion," *Halifax Chronicle*, 26 October 1942. (Miscellaneous Manuscripts Collection. NSARM.)

_____. "Splendid Fellows Maroons," *Halifax Chronicle*, 21 December 1942. (Miscellaneous Manuscripts Collection. NSARM.)

_____. "Magnificant Army Men," *Halifax Chronicle*, n.d. (Miscellaneous Manuscripts Collection. NSARM.)

Robinson, Carey. *The Fighting Maroons of Jamaica*. Kingston, Jamaica: Collins, 1969.

_____. *The Iron Thorn: The Defeat of the British by the Jamaican Maroons*. Kingston, Jamaica: Kingston Publishers Limited, 1993.

Savary, A.W. *History of the County of Annapolis* (supplement). Toronto: William Briggs, 1913.

Sawh, Gobin. ed. *The Canadian Caribbean Connection: Bridging North and South: History, Influences, Lifestyles*. Halifax, N.S.: Carindo Cultural Association, 1992.

Scarlet, Blue and Gold: The Story of the Soldier in the History of Canada. Halifax: The Army Museum, Halifax Citadel, n.d.

Sheehan, Sean. *Cultures of the World: Jamaica*. New York: Marshall Cavendish, 1994.

Sheldon, Helen. "Archaeological Impact Assessment of Daytona Park, Middle Sackville, N.S." Prepared for Anahid Investments Limited, 19 May 1998. (available from the Nova Scotia Museum, Halifax, N.S.)

Silver, Authur P. "The Maroons in Nova Scotia." In George V. Hay, ed. *Canadian History Readings*. vol. 1. Saint John, N.B.: Barnes, 1900, pp. 183-9.

Simons, A.J. "Hetverval van Surinam," *West Indische Gids*, 15 (1934), p. 30. In Price, *The Guiana Maroons*, p. 9.

Strafford, Ellen, ed. *Flamboyant Canadians*. Toronto: Baxter, 1964.

Sutherland, D.A. "Hartshorne, Lawrence." In Halpenny, v. VI, 1821-1835, pp. 312-4.

Thomas, C.E. "The Work, in Nova Scotia, of the Society for the Propagation of the Gospel in Foreign Parts, 1784 to 1886," *Collections of the Nova Scotia Historical Society*, 38 (1973), 63-90.

Thorne, R.G. *The History of Parliament: The House of Commons, 1790-1820* v. Members, Q-Y, London: Secker and Warburg, 1986.

Tolson, Elsie Churchill. *The Captain, the Colonel and Me. (Bedford, N.S., since 1503)*. Sackville, N.B.: Tribune Press, 1979.

Tratt, Gertrude. "Chamberlain, Theophilus." Halpenny, vol. VI, 1821-1835, pp. 128-30.

Trider, Douglas William. *History of Dartmouth and Halifax Harbour, 1415 to 1800*. vol. 1, 1999.

_____. *The History of the Dartmouth Quakers*. Hantsport, N.S.: Lancelot Press, 1994.

Tufts, Karl H. *A Short History of the Parish of Sackville, N.S.* n.p.: For the Author, n.d.

Tulloch, Judith. "Tonge, William Cottnam." In Halpenny, vol. VI, 1821-1835, pp. 778-83.

Veilleaux, Christine. "Hale, John." In Halpenny, vol. VII, 1836-1850, pp. 372-3.

Vernon, C.W. *Bicentenary Sketches and Early Days of the Church in Nova Scotia*. Halifax, 1910.

Walker, James W. St. G. *The Black Loyalists: The Search for a Promised Land in Nova Scotia and Sierra Leone, 1783-1870*. London: Longman & Dalhousie University Press, 1976.

_____. "The Establishment of a Free Black Community in Nova Scotia, 1783-1840." In Martin L. Kilson and Robert I. Rotberg, eds., *The Africian Diaspora: Interpretive Essays*. Cambridge, Mass./London, Eng.: Harvard University Press, 1976, pp. 205-36.

_____. *A History of the Blacks in Canada: A Study Guide for Teachers and Students.* Hull: Canadian Government Publishing Centre, 1980.

_____, et al. *Identity: The Black Experience in Canada.* Toronto: Ontario Communications Authority and Gage, 1979.

Walker, Joan. "The Royal Mistresses." In Strafford, pp. 19-44.

Williams, Eric. *From Columbus to Castro: The History of the Caribbean. 1492-1969.* New York: Harper and Row, 1970.

Wilson, Ellen G. *The Loyal Blacks.* New York: Capricorn, 1976.

Winks, Robin. *The Blacks in Canada: A History.* Montreal: McGill-Queens University Press, 1971.

Wyse, Akintola G. "The Place of Sierra Leone in African Diaspora Studies." In Ajayi, pp. 107-20.

Young, D. Murray, "Gray, Benjamin Gerrish." In Halpenny, vol. VIII, 1851-1860, pp. 344-6.

APPENDIX I

Maroon Names

The following list of names of the Maroons have been gleaned from the public records and documents. The names with military commissions attached came from Maroon petitions to the government of Jamaica or to that of Great Britain. The reader should be aware that these often changed, ie. captains became majors, and so on. Many of the names came from CO217/74: *An account of Maroon Property embarked with them from Nova Scotia to Sierra Leone* discussed in Appendix II. Because of the variety of spellings of the same name — ie., Jerratt, etc., there may be some instances when a single individual is represented more than once. Other names were drawn from the Ross Diary and again inconsistent spelling poses problems for the researcher. Despite these concerns, this is one of the more complete lists of the names of the Maroons who came to Nova Scotia in 1796 and made the journey to Sierra Leone in 1800. Those who were listed as residents of the Maroon community of Boydville in 1800 are specified. Most of the others would have been located in Maroon Town (Preston) prior to their embarkation.

?, Eve
?, Sue
Anglin, Private Wlm.
Baelie, Bonny
Bailey, Barnet
Bailey, Barney
Bailey, Dido
Bailie, Major
Baillie, Nash (Boydville)
Baily, Nanny
Baily, Venus
Baret or [Barnet], Godwin G.
    (Boydville)
Barne, Samuel
Barnet, William
Barnet, Yago
Barnett, Hugh
Barrell, George (Boydville)
Barret [Barnet], Captain James
Barrett, Edward
Bayley, Captain Sam.
Bernard [Bonard],Lieutenant Chas.
Bernard, Lieutenant Daniel
Bernard, Private Jimmy
Bonard [Bernard], Jas.
Bonard, Daniel
Bonard, David

Bonard, Nancy
Bonard, William (Boydville)
Brown, Bob
Brown, James
Brown, Jy.
Brown, Robert
Brown, Tom
Buchnor, David
Buchnor, John
Bucknor, Cuffee
Bucknor, Private Jno.
Bucknor, Tom
Bussia, John (Boydville)
Cameron, Thomas
Camobell, Peter
Campbell, Betsy
Campbell, Private John
Campbell, Thomas
Chambers, Charles
Chambers, Polly
Cooper, Private Daniel
Cuffee, Private Little
Davidson, John
Downer, Captain Robt.
Downer, Casgit (Boydville)
Downing, Chs. (Boydville)
Dunbar, Captain

Dunbar, James
Dunbar, M.
Dunbar, Sally
Dunn, James
Elis, Ann
Elliot, Cantiny
Ellis, B.
Ellis, Betsy
Ellis, C.
Ellis, G.
Ellis, John
Ellis, W.
Forbes, Alex.
Forbes, B.
Forbes, William
Fowler, Robert (Boydville)
Gale, Richard
Garding, Arthur
George, Robert
Gerard, Herbert (Boydville)
Goodwin, Genny
Goodwin, Jenny
Gordon, Privat Peter
Grav [Gray?], Robt.
Gray, Benjamin
Gray, Captain Robt.
Gray, Peggy
Hamilton, Nash
Hardin, Bowen
Hardin, John
Hardin, Nancy
Harding, Boyse
Harding, D.
Harding, N.
Harding, Private Jno.
Harding, Private Quaco
Harding, Thomas
Heath, Dick
Heath, Michael
Heath, MissD.
Heath, Richard
Horton, Sam
Howard, Charles (Boydville)
Hubert, Private John
Inez, Robert
James, Captain Will

James, Col. Montague
James, Private John
James, Samuel
Jarett [Jarrett], Capt. John
Jarrett, Hobard
Jarrett, Jack
Jarrett, Private Robt.
Jarrett, Elsy.
Jerratt [Jarrett], Nancy
Jerratt [Jarrett], Sally
Jerratt [Jarrett], Tom
Jerratt, Herbert
Jerratt, Hert. (Boydville)
Jerratt[Jarrett], Elsy
Johnston, Becky
Johnston[e] [Johnson], Capt.
    Thomas
Johnstone, Jacob
Johnstone, Robin
Lawrence, Captain George
    (Boydville)
Lawrence, Captain James (Boydville)
Lawrence, Tobie (Boydville)
Lawrence, Toby
Leburque, Quaco (Boydville)
Leburt, John (Boydville)
Libert, Private Wlm.
Linton, John
Linton, Kitty
Malcom, Geoe.
Mason, Richard
Matheson, Gilbert
McFarguhar (sic), Geo.
McFarguhar, Kitty
Moira, John
Moody, Taylor (Boydville)
Morgan, John
Morgan, Thomas
Morrison, Archy
Murry, John (Boydville)
O'Connor, Patrick (Boydville)
Ouarrell [Quarrell"], William Daws
    [Dawes?]
Palmer, James (Boydville)
Palmer, Old Captain (Boydville)
Palmer, Private Jno.

Palmer, Tom
Parkinson, Bert
Parkinson, Private Jno.
Parkinson, Thomas, 2nd
Quarrell [Ouarrell], William Daws
    [Dawes?]
Reid, Henry
Reid, Thos.
Rickell (sic), John
Rickett, John
Riely [?], Lieutenant Jas.
Rily [?], J.
Rushe, John (Boydville)
Rushin, I.
Russie, Nancy
Ryan, James
Salmon, Sueky (Boydville)
Samuel, Jack
Samuel[s], Charles (Boydville)
Sarjeant, Edward
Sarjeant, S.
Scarlet, William
Senior, Robert
Sewell, Bessy
Sewell, Nelly
Sewell, Sam
Shane, Charles
Shaw, David
Shaw, Lt. Charles
Shaw, Samuel
Shaw. Captain Sam.
Simpson, Private John

Singer, Robert
Smith, Coup
Smith, Lt. Andrew
Smith, Thomas
Stone, Hutchins
Stone, John (old)
Stone, Phibe
Stone, SamTerrato, Major John
Tharpe [Thorpe], John
Tharpe [Thorpe], Private Saml.
Thomoson, Polly
Thompson, John
Thompson, Lieutenant Jno.
Thorpe, Jno
Thorpe, R.
Thorpe, T.
Tolley, (?)
Tracy, Tom
Webb, Richard
Wheeton, (?)
Whitter, John
Williams, Cyrus
Williams, F.
Williams, Fanny
Williams, Herbert
Williams, James, 1st
Williams, James, 2nd
Williams, Joseph
Wisdom, Ann
Wotters [?], Private Robert
Wright, Robert
Zuaco, Private Little

A P P E N D I X   I I

An Account of Maroon Property embarked with
from Nova Scotia to Sierra Leone: CO 217/74

This document is one of the more useful records of the Maroon community. It contains the names, among others, of at least the heads of households and accordingly will be of interest to genealogical researchers. It also supports Mavis Campbell's discussion about the small number of African names among the Maroons at this period. She points out that only three, "Quaco Harding, Little Quaco, and Little Coffee, still retained half of their names African." (Fighting Maroons, p.251, n.1. Also see Campbell, *The Maroons of Jamaica*, pp.255 and 292, notes 8 and 9.)

It is also an interesting account because an analysis of it helps to reveal both the wealth of the community and the relative wealth of individuals within it. The 550 Maroons received on board the *Asia*, after retaining the personal items they felt they needed for their comfort during the voyage to Africa, stowed in the hold 336 packages containing their wearing apparel and other goods and chattels, as well as three boxes of iron shovels, hoes and hinges and five containers of "necessaries and stoves for the aged and infirm" for their use in Sierra Leone. (Campbell, *Fighting Maroons*, p.162).

However, the document is also very frustrating because of what it does not reveal. It is not very helpful if one is attempting to untangle the family relationships of the 151 men, 177 women, and 222 children who emigrated from Nova Scotia in August of 1800 bound for Sierra Leone. It is even less revealing about the wider kinship ties among the Maroon families and questions about individuals age, occupation, health, and so on, remain unanswered. It is also frustrating in that it hints at without confirming a family based extra-generational leadership hierarchy. For example, among the residents of Boydville was James Palmer, the wartime leader and noted warrior, and Old Captain Palmer. No connection, however, as likely as it might seem, is made between the two and thereby again silencing the hopes of the researcher. But despite this silence, we can tell that Colonel Montague had some thirteen packages of personal possessions stowed away while Sueky Salmon packed only 1 petticoat, 4 shifts, 4 shirts, 2 pairs of breeches, 2 vests, 6 handkerchiefs, 1 pair of stockings, and her bed in anticipation of their use in her future home in Africa.

A comparison of this document with the 13 August 1796 order of "Sundry Articles required to be imported from England for the use of the Maroons" (CO 217/67) suggests both the source of some of the items later transported to Sierra Leone as well as the fact that these were in some cases supplemented and in other cases depleted in the intervening four years. For example, 150 blue duffel great-coats were ordered in 1796 and 337 items of outer wear including coats, jackets, cloaks, and waist-coats were stored and shipped in 1800. Likewise, 25 dozen (300) caps had arrived and 330 left, while 50 dozen

(600) handkerchiefs were ordered and an astounding 1743 were packed away to await their owners in Sierra Leone. Not everything was either so constant or grew in number so dramatically. Of the 25 dozen milled yarn mittens ordered, only 9 pairs are recorded as packed and likewise of the 1000 pairs of hose procured some 600 pairs were landed in Africa. In both cases, however, the normal wear and tear of four winters in Nova Scotia and the awareness that mittens and stockings were not likely to be part of their future in Africa could have led to the reduced numbers packed for use there.

The document does help us to visualize the Maroons in Nova Scotia in the years 1796-1800. While no trousers, shirts, gowns, petticoats, shifts, or aprons had been ordered in 1796, several thousand yards of material, 160 pounds of thread, over 14,000 buttons, and 200 thimbles were provided. The blue duffel great-coats lined with red, the 2000 yards of white flannel ordered for shirts, the blue and red baize, and the 2500 yards of "stout blue Pennystone", paints a colourful picture of the Maroons. The extra 787 shirts, 1095 gowns, 1034 petticoats, 761 shifts and 895 pairs of trousers packed for the voyage to Africa are also likely a testament to the industry of the maroon women.

Much of the rest of the approximately 50 different items that formed the cargo, including the kitchen ware and the tools, can also be traced to the 1796 order. However, in both cases either the quantities had been greatly depleted or an unlikely number had been held back for use on the voyage itself. For example, under 500 of the 4000 pieces of flatware, two of the 488 gimblets, 182 of the 360 hoes, three of the 144 hammers, and only 36 buttons were transported. However, the continued existence of at least 547 of the 600 pairs of shoes procured in 1796 and the increase of the number of blankets from 100 pairs to at least 635 may point to their importance to the Maroons.

The fact that the possessions of the Boydville Maroons were certified by a different official than were those at Preston makes a straight comparison of the two groups difficult. The Boydville community consisted of eighteen family units, seventeen headed by a male and one by a female. The seventeen males represent 11% of the total adult male Maroons while the estimate of about 60 persons in Boydville is again 11% of the entire Maroon community. The clothes packed in the hold of the *Asia* by the Boydville settlers was roughly equal to their percentage of the total population with some minor exceptions. For example, the 11% of the population that were from Boydville owned 17.5% of the coats, 17.7% of the shirts, 8% of the handkerchiefs, and 6.7% of the vests. However, they held a disproportional 18.8% of the flatware, 18.6% of the cooking utensils, 15.1% of the blankets, 13.6% of the flat irons, and all of the tools including, hoes, hammers, bill hooks, shovels, and gimblets. However, not one of the 73 boxes of trinkets shipped belonged to the Boydville Maroons.

This suggests that the small Boydville community was slightly, but likely not remarkably, more prosperous than their Maroon Town counterparts. Prosperity of course of any degree was not evenly spread across the community. Some families, like those of John Ellis, Michl. Heath, Col. Montague, Charles Shaw, and Andrew Smith of Preston or Toby Lawrence of Boydville seem to have accumulated more of the worlds treasures than did the families of many of their fellows including Robert George and Nancy Bonard. The community thus revealed by this document was one that economically was not very different than the larger Nova Scotia community of which it was a part.

The full version of the Account of Maroon Property can be seen on the author's website (www.stfx.ca — follow links to John Grant at School of Education).

INDEX

INDEX

AGMV Marquis

MEMBER OF SCABRINI MEDIA

Quebec, Canada
2002